PAINTINGS GALLERY DRESDEN

Newsweek / GREAT MUSEUMS OF THE WORLD

NEW YORK, N.Y.

**GREAT MUSEUMS
OF THE WORLD**

Editorial Director — Carlo Ludovico Ragghianti
American Editor — Henry A. LaFarge

PAINTINGS GALLERY DRESDEN

Introduction by:
Manfred Bachmann

Critical texts by:
Licia Collobi Ragghianti
Gigetta Dalli Regoli
Raffaele Monti
Pier Carlo Santini
Ranieri Varese

Editor-in-chief:
Mariella de Battisti

Design:
Fiorenzo Giorgi

Published by
NEWSWEEK, INC.
& ARNOLDO MONDADORI EDITORE

This volume is being published simultaneously under the
title of *The Splendors of Dresden*

INTRODUCTION

Manfred Bachmann, *General Director*
Dresden Paintings Gallery

Opinion is still divided over the exact date when the Dresden *Alte Meister*, or old masters collection, was established as a picture gallery. By 1707 there was already a collection of paintings which formed part of the *Kunstkammer*, or small "cabinet of art treasures" begun by the Elector Augustus I of Saxony (1526-1586), in his castle around 1560, of which the jeweler Tobias Beutel possessed an inventory. At this time five hundred and thirty-five paintings were chosen to decorate the state rooms of the castle in Dresden, among which were Rubens' *Drunken Hercules* and Giorgione's and Titian's *Sleeping Venus*.

However, 1722 is the generally accepted date for the actual founding of the *Gemäldegalerie* or Paintings Gallery. In that year the Elector-Prince Augustus II, known as Augustus the Strong (1670-1733), ordered an inventory of all the paintings then in his possession, and transferred them to the Stallhof of the Judenhof, the stables built by Paul Buchner between 1586 and 1588, which had been altered for this use. Further alterations were undertaken between 1744 and 1746 on the orders of the Elector-Prince Frederick Augustus III (1696-1763) when, in order to improve the lighting, the large arched windows which can be seen in the view of the Neumarkt painted by Bernardo Bellotto were cut in the façade [see page 68].

The inventory drawn up by the "secret servant" Steinhauser between 1722 and 1728 (listing one thousand nine hundred and ninety-five objects) is still in the archives of the *Gemäldegalerie*, available as an important source of original documentary information. By establishing this gallery Augustus the Strong was carrying out the suggestion of the Court's head architect Raymond Le Plat, a man of wide experience and imagination who held that an art collection was appropriate to the needs of a prince's residence. It appears therefore that in the first ten years of the eighteenth century there was already established in Dresden a separate collection of paintings—whether or not it could yet be called the *Gemäldegalerie*—which grew out of the *Kunstkammer*. There were, besides, other princely collections which became established in succeeding years: the Print Collection, in 1720; the *"Grünes Gewolbe"* between 1721 and 1724; the fitting out of the Dutch Palace for porcelains in 1723 (later called "Japanese Palace" and later known as the *Porzellansschloss*, or Porcelain Castle); and finally the Collection of Antiquities, in 1728. This was the way in which the dismemberment of the old *Kunstkammer* took place, a process which was not concluded until 1831.

Even by the death of Augustus the Strong in 1733 the *Gemäldegalerie* contained an excellent collection of pictures. But it was to be during the reign of his son, Frederick Augustus III of Saxony, later King of Poland, that the gallery came to acquire a world-wide importance. On all the centers of the European art market, from Venice to Paris, and from Prague to Amsterdam, droves of Saxon agents and dealers were unleashed to deal for their sovereign, who, after rising to the throne in 1733 appeared to take little interest in the affairs of state, absorbed by his overriding passion for collecting.

The work of the various agents and dealers was co-ordinated by the Saxon Prime Minister, Count Heinrich von Brühl. Brühl was an ambiguous character, dominated by an uncompromising thirst for personal power. With the help and advice of Carl Heinrich von Heinecken, the collection's curator and the creator of the collection of prints in addition to being his private secretary, Brühl built up his own personal collection of paintings, which was acquired after his death by Catherine the Great of Russia for the Hermitage in St. Petersburg (1769).

Born as a reflection of an inordinate desire for political power and the wish to create an im-

9

pression of princely grandeur in the minds of "ambassadors and other distinguished foreigners" (Brühl), the Dresden collection served to emphasize the luxury of the Saxon court—modeled on that of Louis XIV at Versailles—and at the same time to symbolize the figure of the absolute monarch. Its economic base rested above all on Saxony's production and trade deriving from the mining industry, and the levying of taxes whose heavy weight fell on the shoulders of the working classes, to whom the treasures of the collection of course remained inaccessible.

Among the most important of the early acquisitions was Giorgione's *Sleeping Venus* (finished by Titian), bought in 1699 with fourteen other paintings from the Parisian art dealer Charles Le Roy. Also significant were one hundred of the best paintings from the famous collection of Duke Francesco III of Modena (1746), among which there were four Correggio altarpieces, the four Veronese paintings executed for the Palazzo Cuccina in Venice, Titian's *Tribute Money*, and Hans Holbein the Younger's portrait of *Charles de Solier, Sieur de Morette*. In the inventory of the Wallenstein collection in Dux (comprising two hundred and sixty-eight works), acquired through the intervention of the court painter Johann Gottfried Riedel, were works by Vermeer, Frans Hals and van Dyck; and from part of the Imperial collection in Prague, came the series of "Parable" paintings by Domenico Feti, Valentin de Boullogne's *The Card Players* and Rubens' *The Boar Hunt*. From Paris there came, among other paintings, the *Self-Portrait with Saskia* and *Saskia Holding a Carnation* by Rembrandt, the *Mercury and Argos* by Rubens, Poussin's *Pan and Syrinx* and a number of Wouwerman's works. Particular recognition is due to Count Francesco Algarotti (1712-1764), a brilliant representative of eighteenth-century Enlightenment, for obtaining many of the gallery's important acquisitions. These were principally Italian paintings, including works by Bernardo Strozzi, Palma the Elder, Piazzetta and Sebastiano Ricci, not to mention the *Chocolate Girl* by Liotard, bought in Paris in 1746 from the artist himself. In that year it was decided to frame the paintings, giving the collection a greater sense of uniformity and unity. Toward the end of this golden period, which established the collection's basic character, came the acquisition of Raphael's *Sistine Madonna*, which, after long and difficult negotiations carried on in Piacenza and concluded with the payment of the considerable sum of twenty thousand ducats, arrived in Dresden between 1753 and 1754.

The outbreak of the Seven Years War, whose political and economic effects were to have severe financial repercussions in Saxony, signaled the end of the policy of collecting on a grand scale. In 1759 many of the paintings were taken to the castle of Königstein, and some of them were irreparably damaged in the process.

An important period in the history of the *Gemäldegalerie* came between 1847 and 1855 with the construction of a special museum designed by Gottfried Semper (1803-1879) in the Italian Renaissance style, contrasting clearly with the Baroque architecture of the Zwinger [the great square of buildings of which it now formed the fourth side]. Semper, called to Dresden in 1834 on the recommendation of F. C. Gau, had already given an indication of considerable talents in the building of the Dresden Opera House; he was also the director of the School of Architecture in the Academy of Fine Arts.

In 1848, at the outbreak of the bourgeois democratic rebellions which were to lead to an armed insurrection in Dresden in May 1849, Semper, along with Richard Wagner and others, took the side of the revolutionaries, and warrants of arrest for high treason were issued against them. Semper had to flee to England, from where, despite his exile, he directed the continuing work of construction; and it was not until 1863 that he was able to return to his country.

Semper's building, which at that time pioneered museum architectural design was completed in 1855 and soon had two thousand two hundred works hanging in it. The installation of these paintings—which was quite different from the old seventeenth-century manner of hanging pictures—was made the responsibility of Julius Schnorr von Carolsfeld (1749-1872). Like his successor Julius Hübner (1806-1882), Schnorr was a professor at Dresden's Academy of Fine Arts and belonged to that class of painter-directors who were so common in the museum circles of the nineteenth century.

It was only with Karl Woermann (1847-1933), who became Director in 1882, that the running of the *Gemäldegalerie* was finally made the responsibility of a scholar and art-historian. To his work we owe the compilation of a general critical catalogue (the first edition came out in 1887) which still provides the basis for any new study or catalogue of the works in the gallery. The systematic examination of the paintings led to many new attributions, and to many famous attributions being discredited.

At that time the care and conservation of the paintings also became an object of attention. In 1836 a committee, later to become a commission, was formed, with, among other things, the task of dealing with the problems relative to conservation and restoration. Already a few years before, in 1826, the Italian Pietro Palmaroli had been called to Dresden to restore a number of important works, one of which was Raphael's *Sistine Madonna*. Palmaroli completed his job with efficiency and ability, going on to tackle the new task of setting up a local and independent school of restoration.

Up until the middle of the eighteenth century only the royal family, the court, and a few other special people were privileged to admire the masterpieces of the *Gemäldegalerie*. Even Johann Joachim Winckelmann, considered to be the founder of modern art-history, had great difficulty in gaining entrance. In the second half of the eighteenth century it became possible for foreign travelers to visit the collection, but only upon payment of a large tip. At this time, to meet the needs of the "upper classes," Riedel and the keeper of the Print Collection Wenzel published, in French, the museum's first catalogue (1765). The first German edition followed in 1771.

Although the change from absolute to constitutional monarchy in 1831 led to the nationalization of the collection, in the middle years of the century it was still in effect impossible for the lower classes, the farm laborers, artisans and workers, to visit the galleries; in fact an order in 1839 gave notice that the museum was open on working days between 9:00 A.M. and 1:00 P.M. to "well dressed" persons. This ruling could only benefit the middle classes and rich pensioners.

It was only in 1931 that the *Gemäldegalerie Neue Meister* (Gallery of Modern Masters) became an individual entity independent of the *Gemäldegalerie Alte Meister* (Gallery of Old Masters), although it remained for a long time—until 1945—under the control of the same director as the *Alte Meister*. The outbreak of the Second World War put a stop to plans for a new building. From 1925 until 1931 the works belonging to the new department had been hung in the "Palais" on the Parkstrasse, while between 1931 and the War the department moved to the Secundogenitur on the Brühlisehen Terrasse, where the nineteenth-century works enjoyed a very congenial setting.

The Impressionist and Post-Impressionist paintings—which Dresden had the opportunity to admire at the 1926 International Exhibition, and bought a certain number for the *Gemäldegalerie*—were hung in the place now occupied by the historical collection, the east wing of

Semper's building. Between 1946 and 1965 the collection was provisionally housed in Pillnitz Castle. In 1959 it was given a fully autonomous status and called the *Gemäldégalerie Neue Meister*. Since October 20, 1965, when the nineteenth- and twentieth-century masterpieces— enriched by important pieces of sculpture of the same period from the Sculpture Collection— were moved into the skylight-lit galleries of the Albertinum (a former arsenal), it has been possible for visitors to have a complete picture of the development of art during the last two centuries.

The Gallery of Modern Masters, which developed from a department in the old *Gemäldegalerie* devoted to nineteenth-century art, was born in answer to middle-class cultural tastes, under the influence of the bourgeois democratic revolution of 1848-49. Its beginnings are closely connected with the work of the liberal politician Bernhard August von Lindenau (1779-1854). He was among the authors of the first Saxon Constitution and civil code which was, for its time, very progressive. President of the Council of Ministers from 1831, Lindenau was forced in 1843 to give way to his political rival, the reactionary von Konneritz. Lindenau had stipulated that his pension should be spent for the promotion of the arts and sciences, and part of the sum went towards financing acquisitions for the *Gemäldegalerie*. In 1848 Lindenau's gift was supplemented by the academic council, which had control over both the Academy of Fine Arts and the *Gemäldegalerie*. Its members decided that from then on half the profits from the exhibitions organized by the Academy should be made available for acquisitions of works of art for the museum. The norms by which the paintings were chosen suggested that they should be by "national artists, if possible still living." By the term "national" it was understood that they should be Saxon artists. It was only under the direction of the art historian Karl Woermann, from 1882 onwards, that this narrow policy was abandoned in favor of a more farsighted one which would be of greater benefit for the future of the *Gemäldegalerie*.

After a history full of changes the Gallery of Modern Masters today consists of five main sections: German romanticism and late romanticism; bourgeois nineteenth-century realism; Impressionist painting, followed by Expressionism and the movements associated with it; proletarian revolutionary art; contemporary Socialist art from the German Democratic republic, the Soviet Union and the socialist countries.

The war unleashed by Hitler's Germany put Dresden's art treasures in grave danger. Already by a few days before the outbreak of hostilities in 1939 the complete dispersal of the collections had been planned. In the second half of 1942, under the combination of pressure from the few remaining experts and the increasingly acute danger from bombing raids, the removal of works of art to places considered safer began, that is to castles and country houses scattered through forty-five different places in Saxony. On February 13, 1945, in the rain of bombs of the Anglo-American aerial attack, fifteen square kilometers of the old city center were razed to the ground; various museum buildings, as well as some world-famous monuments, were reduced to ruins. In the process, forty-two large-size paintings were lost by fire in Dresden Castle, in addition to another hundred and fifty-four which had been loaded onto a covered lorry parked on the banks of the river, near the Terrassenufer. As the fighting approached the German borders at the beginning of 1945, in the face of heavy blows inflicted by the Soviet Union on the Nazi war machine, the Nazi leaders—right in the middle of the winter—issued the criminal order to transfer from the east to the west of the Elbe all the works which had been recovered. As a result the masterpieces, which until then had been stored in a more or less well-ordered manner, ended up in completely unsuitable shelters such as the limestone quarries of Pockan-Lengefeld and the tunnel in the sandstone quarry of Rottwendorf. The paintings and precious objects of the collection were thus exposed to the danger of severe deterioration. The Nazi despots had still another aim; to set aside the masterpieces and pull them out of the reach of the Soviet forces so as to be able after the war to use them for speculation and making deals. Martin Mutschmann, the commander-in-chief of the Nazi forces in Saxony, acutally gave the order to blow up the masterpieces of the *Gemäldegalerie* before he fled. At least two hundred and six paintings were destroyed in the fighting. The catalogue of missing works, compiled in 1963 by Hans Ebert, lists another five hundred and seven lost works whose fate is still unknown today. Thanks to an immense amount of research it has been possible to trace some of these lost paintings and return them to the collection.

In 1945 seven hundred and sixty-two of the Gallery's paintings were temporarily sent to Moscow, another four hundred and seventy-eight to Kiev; and the remainder went to Leningrad. Here they were also partly restored: in all one thousand two hundred and forty works, which in 1955 returned to Dresden, followed in 1958 by all the artistic patrimony of the German museums which had until then been preserved in the Soviet Union, among which were the treasures of six other Dresden collections. The war had inflicted heavy damages on the other art museums as well; and that was on top of the 1937 Nazi campaign against *"Entartete Kunst"* ("Degenerate Art") which had resulted in the removal of altogether four hundred and thirty-seven works from the *Neue Meister*, the Print and Sculpture collections.

With the entrance of the Red Army into Dresden on May 8, 1945 the hundred and fifty-fourth Battalion of the Fifth Army of the First Ukrainian Front, under the command of Major Perevostcikov, had been given the order to trace and salvage the "evacuated" art treasures. In the face of great difficulties the officers and soldiers, as well as the technicians, scholars, restorers and artists assigned to the salvage operation, fulfilled their task in an exemplary manner. After being recovered the works of art found a temporary refuge in the museums of Moscow, Kiev and Leningrad where they were placed in the conscientious care of our Soviet colleagues; seven hundred and sixty-two of the *Gemäldegalerie's* paintings ended up in Moscow, four hundred and seventy-eight in Kiev.

Raphael's *Sistine Madonna* is for us an expression and symbol of the exalted ethical ideals of Renaissance culture, produced by the progressive bourgeois classes of the Italian cities. Michael W. Alpatow has described the *Sistine Madonna* as being one of the most elevated, profound and poetically forceful examples of Renaissance painting. This painting, so expressive of the gentle dignity of motherhood and the fascination of woman, occupies a special place in the memoirs and writings of many famous visitors and other art lovers to the *Gemäldegalerie*. Today it still draws the attention of the millions of visitors to the *Gemäldegalerie*; it has become practically a symbol of the dramatic recovery of Dresden's artistic treasures by the Soviet army.

The salvaging of these masterpieces by the Red Army, the careful operation of conservation and restoration in the Soviet Union until their return to the newly rebuilt museums in Dresden, the experience gained from Russian museums and the exchange exhibitions (constantly being increased by "pacts of friendship") convincingly illustrate the fraternal links between our peoples.

In a solemn ceremony in 1955 which took place in the Pushkin Museum the Soviet Government celebrated the return to Dresden of the one thousand two hundred and forty works from the *Gemäldegalerie* which had been recovered. Later, in 1958, all the collections belonging to museums of the German Democratic Republic which had been preserved in the USSR were returned, among which there were also the treasures from another six Dresden collections.

By a decree of the Democratic Republic of June 1955—a hundred years after the completion of Semper's museum—work began on the reconstruction of the building, which had been badly damaged by the bombs on the night of February 13, 1945. Up until the completion of the first part of the restoration, the paintings were hung—from May to August 1955—in the Pushkin Museum in Moscow, and from November 1955 until April 1956 in the National Gallery in Berlin. On June 3, 1956, it was already possible to re-open the central and eastern parts of the museum, after a commemorative speech by the head of state Otto Grotewohl, at the end of the celebrations marking the 750th anniversary of the founding of the city. On October 31, 1960, the *Gemäldegalerie*, now completely rebuilt, was finally re-opened in its entirety after a speech by its Director, Henner Menz, during the celebrations marking the 400th anniversary of the Dresden art collection. As the "home" of world-famous paintings, the collection testifies to the diligence and farsightedness of its builders, and Dresden once more returned to the ranks of the most beautiful art capitals in the world. Those who worked on the building, together with the architects Frenzel and Zimmerman, merited great praise for their share in the reconstruction of the *Gemäldegalerie Alte Meister*.

Already in the nineteenth century the more progressive elements of the bourgeoisie were, like Gottfried Semper (1803-1879), demanding that the doors of the collection should be opened to the people and that the works of art should be used "as a very efficient means of national education." It is only under the German Democratic Republic that these aims have been fully achieved. Today the eleven museums of the state collections of art in Dresden are visited by two and a half million people a year.

In 1978, out of roughly half a million people living in Dresden, more than 90,000, mostly workers from the city's cooperatives, held annual season tickets allowing them free entry into the museums. The number of guided visits is also large, and with the help of tape-recorders these can be organized in eighteen different languages.

As in the other State art collections, the workers have become a creative partner in the *Gemäldegalerie*, both of the Old Masters and of the Modern Masters. A series of enterprises have helped decisively in strengthening the close ties between artists and the working classes. Socialist brigades, state cooperatives and units from the People's Army have had their "cultural baptism" through participating in the artistic events at the *Gemäldegalerie*. There are in addition special guided tours and exhibitions for the workers from local state cooperatives, concerts in the museums and other activities aimed at the schools, in collaboration with the youth organizations; also competitions for students, "Museum Days" for young workers, not to mention the lively exchange of interests between the Youth Club and Pioneer's 25 Club, and the many activities organized by the "Circle of Friends of the Gallery of Modern Masters." Scholarly catalogues of the reserve collections and special exhibitions, guides published in various languages, the *Dresdner Kunstblatter* and *Jahrbuch*, and the monthly programmes of events which have a high circulation, all serve to spread detailed information and publish the results of the latest research.

Since Semper's museum was reopened, special loan exhibitions from both the *Alte* and *Neue Meister* [Old and Modern Masters] have traveled to many places including Belgrade, Budapest, Bucharest, Leningrad, Minsk, Moscow, Prague, Sofia, Tokyo and Kyoto. In the comprehensive exhibitions of the State art collections which took place in Stockholm (1969), Zürich (1971) and the United States (1978-1979), both parts of the *Gemäldegalerie*, the *Alte Meister* and the *Neue Meister*, were well represented. The *Alte Meister* has sent more than three hundred works to joint exhibitions shared with other socialist countries in cities outside the German Democratic Republic. Since 1957 the *Alte Meister* has either mounted or participated in many special exhibitions which have been very important in the field of research. These include *Bernardo Bellotto* (1964); *Venetian Painting from the Fifteenth to the Eighteenth Century* (1968); *William Turner* (1970); *German Art in Dürer's Time* and *The Birth of the New Man* (1971); *The Gemäldegalerie Alte Meister's new acquisitions for the German Section* (1974); *Two Hundred Years of Painting in Dresden* (1976). In 1972, the museum's anniversary year, two exhibitions were organized: *Painters in Dresden in the 19th and 20th Centuries* and *European Landscape Painting 1550-1650*. The 1974 exhibition, *Caspar David Friedrich and his School,* was of international importance.

The *Gemäldegalerie Neue Meister* primarily supports and patronizes the Socialist Realism of the German Democratic Republic and the other Socialist countries, both with a full programme of special exhibitions which also travel to other parts of the country, and with an active policy of acquisitions. This is particularly useful in recording Dresden's art history. The friendly relations with the major art collections of the Soviet Union and the other Socialist countries have led to a closer international collaboration and a widening of the subjects offered by the two collections. So that, in 1968, the Gallery of Modern Masters was able to hold, among others, the exhibition *Serbian Painting between the two World Wars, 1918-1939* and in 1969 the first large exhibition of Georgian twentieth-century painting, drawing and sculpture.

In 1972, on the occasion of the two hundred and fiftieth anniversary of the *Gemäldegalerie Alte Meister*, there were some very good exhibitions of works from Soviet museums at the Albertinum, notably *Masterpieces of the Hermitage in Leningrad—Brühl Collection*. The twentieth anniversary of the reopening of the *Gemäldegalerie*, in 1976, was marked by the very well received exhibition of *Masterpieces of French Painting of the 19th and 20th Centuries*, these also coming from the Museums of Moscow and Leningrad. The thirtieth anniversary of the liberation of the German people from the Nazis by the Soviet Union provided the occasion for the first joint show by the Artist's Union (*Künstlerverbande*) of Dresden and Leningrad, which took place in those two cities.

In a coherent realization of the ideals of Socialist political culture, the German Democratic Republic has created modern museums for Dresden's famous art treasures, and united the old reconstructed cultural centers with the new residential centers on the banks of the Elbe.

Dresden, a flourishing city with a working class enriched by a revolutionary tradition, dynamic industry, numerous scientific institutes and universities, interesting historic buildings and natural beauty, a center for the activities of famous artists and scholars, has also become for the first time in its history a vital and lasting center for bringing art to the working people.

ITALIAN PAINTING
14th-18th Centuries

MASTER OF THE LIVELY CHILD (GHERARDO STARNINA?). *Madonna.*
This painting was originally part of a triptych commissioned by Cardinal Pietro Corsini for the San Lorenzo chapel in the cathedral of Florence. Other surviving parts of the original are preserved in the Boymans van Beuningen Museum in Rotterdam, the Berlin State Museums, and the National Gallery of Stockholm.

Up to the present day critics have remained divided in their identification of the author, evidently an artist of great refinement who is generally known as the Master of the Lively Child. Some see him as Gherardo Starnina, who was active in Italy and Spain and played an important role in the International Gothic movement; others as the Spaniard Miguel Alcaniz, one of Starnina's collaborators when he returned to Italy. The figure of the Virgin, cut down and damaged as it is, reflects in every detail a marked taste for decorative effects. This can be seen in the treatment of the large crown and the halo set against the gilded background, and the delicate white veil which encircles the Madonna's neck, separating the head from the body and contrasting with the sumptuous brocade of her dress. The prevailing curvilinear rhythms, extended to the whole triptych in its original state, created a network of links between the Madonna, the angels, the saints, and the donor. (G.D.R.)

MASTER OF THE LIVELY CHILD
(GHERARDO STARNINA?)
Active in the last years of the fourteenth century and first years of the fifteenth century.
Madonna (surviving detail of the original painting), ca. 1422
Tempera on panel; 13¾" x 11½".
Inv. no. 30

LORENZO DI CREDI (?)
Florence ca. 1456—Florence 1537
Portrait of a Youth (ca. 1480–1490)
Tempera and oil (?) on panel; 19¾" x 14"
Inv. no. 41
Behind the figure to the right is visible a low stone parapet indicating that the young man is indoors, in front of an open window or on a balcony. In an inventory of 1722 this work was listed as a copy of a work by Raphael.

LORENZO DI CREDI. *Portrait of a Youth.*   *p. 19*

This portrait of a boyish youth with a sulky expression was for a long time tentatively attributed to Pinturicchio. Recent studies by C. L. Ragghianti have thrown more light on the subject, linking this work with a more famous portrait in the Uffizi, presumed to be of Verrocchio. This latter work has always been attributed to either Credi, Perugino or the young Raphael.

The brushwork technique employed in this painting, namely the variation in tone achieved by using "brushes of different types and thicknesses" which leave visible traces of the thickness of the impasto, is exactly similar to methods used by Credi in his drawings on tinted paper, in particular in his studies of heads. These he often throws into relief by using thick brushstrokes of white lead. There are elements of similarity with Credi's work too in the way the landscape is treated: bright spots of color (highlights) are used to make various elements stand out; and the towers of the town rising in the background between the river and the trees has an exact counterpart in an example of Credi's work in the Uffizi Cabinet of Drawings and Prints. (G.D.R.)

SANDRO BOTTICELLI (ALESSANDRO DI MARIANO FILIPEPI)
Florence 1444/1445—Florence 1510
Scenes from the Life of St. Zenobius: Last Miracle and Death of the Saint (1495–1500)
Tempera on panel; 26″ x 71⅛″.
Inv. no. 9
The cycle consists of four panels which were probably painted for a Florentine confraternity, since the cult of St. Zenobius, Bishop of Florence, was widespread in the city. It is suggested that the patrons may have been the society named after the Saint.
The first and second panels passed from the hands of the Rondinelli family in Florence to the Mond Collection in London in 1891. In 1924 they were left to the National Gallery in London. The third panel passed from Florence to Milan and subsequently Berlin. At the beginning of the present century it was in the Abdy collection in London, from where it was sold in 1911 to the Metropolitan Museum of New York. The fourth and last panel formed part of the Metzger Collection in Florence in the last century from where it passed to the von Quandt Collection in Dresden and thence to the Gallery.

SANDRO BOTTICELLI. *Scenes from the Life of St. Zenobius: Last Miracle and Death of the Saint.*

According to Vasari, the four panels which make up this series were probably painted "*per ricignimento e spalliera*" ("as part of the furniture") i.e. specifically for some room being fitted out with a special purpose in mind. Botticelli painted series of this sort for the Vespucci and Pucci families, and Piero di Cosimo did them for the Vespucci and del Pugliese. The most famous example of this genre, however, is probably a series of panels painted in the second decade of the sixteenth century by

20

a group of Florentine artists for the Borgherini-Acciaioli wedding.

The four panels of this series by Botticelli show events from the life of St. Zenobius. They almost all take place in the open air, in a city whose streets, piazzas and loggias are all portrayed in the most rigorously accurate perspective. A few details make it recognizable as Florence but somehow it gives the impression of having been built in a laboratory; the careful measurement of volumes and planes, the way the colors are juxtaposed and the workmanlike accuracy with which the marble, stone, brick and wood are portrayed, all go to create the ideal background for the action of the pictures. Even the clothes, faces and gestures of the people are defined by the demands of the story.

This panel, which is the last in the series, shows a single miracle. It is divided into three episodes to give full force to the different steps in the action. In the first, a child is run down by a heavy cart, and with the despair of all around is picked up, its arms hanging limp, head dropped back and eyes lifeless. Then, in the second scene, Eugenio (Zenobius' deacon) intervenes and restores the child to his family unharmed. The final scene shows the saint, now ill, announcing his own death and taking leave of his followers. (G.D.R.)

DANIELE DA VOLTERRA. *Moses on Sinai.* *p. 22*
The events in this picture depict two separate incidents taking place while the people of Israel were encamped at the foot of Mount Sinai, after their crossing of the Red Sea. The tall cylindrical shape of the mountain itself accentuates the drama of the first incident: God, appearing in the midst of clouds, entrusts the tablets to Moses, while in the distant background at the upper left the people cower back, terrified by the lightning and trumpet blasts.

In the second incident the obscure mass of the mountain also serves to accentuate the most detailed and complex action taking place in the foreground. On coming down from the mountain, Moses finds the Israelites lying prostrate in adoration of the Golden Calf, and in his fury breaks the tablets of the Law. In this particular scene the contorted bodies, the gestures of fear and horror, the desperate faces, the half-naked figures and the rich color and texture of the materials all reflect the degree to which the artist had assimilated the recently developed Mannerist techniques. (G.D.R.)

RAPHAEL. *The Sistine Madonna.* *p. 23*
There is no documentary evidence about the origins of the painting nor do we know whether the monks of the black-robed Order of St. Sixtus in Piacenza commissioned this work for their church directly from the artist or whether they acquired it in Rome. There are in fact several hypotheses, including one that suggests that it came from the tomb of Pope Julius II. But the most likely theory seems to be that the monks at Piacenza did actually commission it themselves and that it was in their church that it first hung. Placed in the apse like a window opening into heaven, the picture would certainly have been ideally situated for its compositional structure.

This structure may at first seem simple because of the limited number of its component parts but closer inspection reveals complex meanings and carefully calculated relationships and divisions of space. The edges of the two curtains draw the attention of the observer towards the figure of the Virgin. Barefoot, without halo, and simply dressed, she holds the child easily and walks forward with a firm light

DANIELE DA VOLTERRA (DANIELE
RICCIARELLI)
Volterra 1509—Rome 1566
Moses on Sinai
Oil on panel; 54¼" x 39⅛".
Inv. no. 87

tread; evidence of this movement can be seen in the way her clothing presses
against her legs and how her cloak billows in the wind. She walks on thick clouds
which provide her with firm, yet at the same time fluid, support. What appear to be
clouds in the background are in fact the faces of a multitude of children—angels
who from far away and high above are watching over the Virgin and Child. On either side, at different levels, kneel St. Sixtus (whose face can be recognized as that
of Julius II delle Rovere) and St. Barbara (who, it has been suggested, resembles
one of the Pope's nieces, either Julia Orsini or Lucrezia delle Rovere). The way Sixtus kneels, and particularly the gesture of his outstretched hand, are intended to in-
volve the onlooker and, ideally, to draw him in. The sill at the base, on which the
papal tiara stands and against which two winged cherubs lean, serves as a sort of
link between the interior of the picture and the external world, and by extension between heaven and earth, the human and the divine. (G.D.R.)

RAPHAEL (RAFFAELLO SANZIO)
Urbino 1483—Rome 1520
The Sistine Madonna (1512–13)
Oil on canvas; 104⅝" x 77⅛".
Inv. no. 93
The Virgin stands with the Holy Child in her
arms between St. Sixtus and St. Barbara. The
painting came originally from the monastery of
St. Sixtus in Piacenza. In 1754 it was sold by the
monks to King Frederick Augustus III of
Saxony and a copy by Nogari was hung in its
place. After the Second World War the original
painting was taken to Moscow, but later
returned to the Dresden Gallery.

24

ANDREA DEL SARTO (ANDREA D'AGNOLO)
Florence 1486—Florence 1530
Sacrifice of Isaac (1527–28)
Oil on panel; 83⅝″ x 62⅝″.
Signed at bottom right with the monogram AA.
Inv. no. 77
Commissioned by Giovanni Battista della Palla for King Francis I of France. The work was perhaps intended to balance the *Carità* by the same artist, originally at Fontainebleau and now in the Louvre. During the sixteenth century it was owned by Filippo Strozzi, who sold it to the Marchese del Vasto for 107 ducats. According to Baldinucci it was taken to Spain and brought back to Florence where it was hung by the Medici in the Uffizi Gallery. After this it was exchanged between Cardinal Carlo de' Medici and the Duke of Modena, from whose gallery it passed into the collection of King Frederick Augustus III of Saxony in 1746, and from there to its present location.

FERRARESE ARTIST OF THE SECOND HALF OF THE FIFTEENTH CENTURY
St. Sebastian (ca. 1480)
Tempera on panel; 68″ x 23″
Inv. no. 42A
Still in Ferrara in the Costabili collection in 1838, the painting was later acquired by the art dealer Guggenheim, who sold it to the Dresden Gallery in 1896.

ANDREA DEL SARTO. *Sacrifice of Isaac.* *p. 24*

Painted for the ambitious and cultivated monarch Francis I and destined for Fontainebleau, which from about that time onwards was to become a center for artistic production, this picture could hardly avoid being a restatement of pictorial components and at the same time very carefully designed. This can be seen in the way the different elements of the picture are perfectly balanced and linked together yet at the same time remaining distinct: the quite obvious evidence of the artist's deep study of classical sculptures, particularly those which had recently come to light such as the Laocöon, discovered on the Esquiline in 1506. There is also a superb mastery of linear perspective (note the quadrangular block on which Isaac leans) and of aerial perspective (the break in the clouds in the background as the sky begins to clear.) Finally, there is the artist's ability to include in his work the heritage of an illustrious iconographic tradition, descending from the panels created by Brunelleschi and Ghiberti more than a century before. (G.D.R.)

FERRARESE ARTIST OF THE SECOND HALF OF THE FIFTEENTH CENTURY. *St. Sebastian.* *p. 25*

The name of Lorenzo Costa in the Hebrew script on the small shield at the base of this painting having been deciphered by the critic Salvatore Anau, the panel has been generally attributed to that artist. One is tempted to explain the style so uncharacteristic of Costa—its old-fashioned, Tura-like qualities—by quoting the commission, which specified a painting "in the style of Tura" (Longhi). This argument, however, seems both complex and artificial, and it appears both simpler and more reasonable to suppose that the authorship of the work may well have been shared. Tura's obvious influence, particularly in the treatment of the architectural elements, is not enough to hide the fact that his dry, expressive power has been watered down into a rather lifeless, schematized composition, divorced from any sense of emotion or vitality. It was probably painted by an old-fashioned Ferrarese artist who, painting towards the end of the century when his contemporaries were looking to Venice and Mantua, was unable to lift his style out of the narrow mold in which it had developed.

Lorenzo Costa's hand can only be attached to the small figure of the soldier holding the standard at St. Sebastian's feet, painted in a style similar to that of the *Argonauts* and some of the figures in the Brera *Adoration*. It is quite possible that Costa added this figure with his signature, though this would have been the extent of his contribution to the whole. (R.V.)

FRANCESCO DEL COSSA. *The Annunciation.*

This panel is one of the most perfect examples of the character and the elements which came to be associated with the "Ferrarese workshop." In an analytical and punctilious manner, Cossa transforms the substance of the composition into precious material. From this there results a kind of abstraction. The painter refuses to simulate reality, to reconstitute nature in a banal, imitative manner. The rare, costly marbles are felt as if they were the stones of Creation, defined in aspect and form for eternity.

The construction of space which binds together the various parts of the composition is based on an assured mastery of the rules of perspective. Nothing is left to chance and one feels throughout the deep conviction of the artist in the way in which every detail is of equal importance and necessary for the pre-determined conclusion. The space in which the Virgin stands at the moment of the Annunciation is closed off in the background by the receding arches which fully define the space of the action.

It has been noted that the snail in the foreground is supposed to have magical connotations; this, however, in no way detracts from the intense realism of Cossa's vision, and is of little relevance to his artistic approach. (R.V.)

FRANCESCO DEL COSSA
Ferrara 1436—Bologna 1478
The Annunciation (1470–72)
Tempera on panel; 54" x 44½".
Inv. no. 43
Executed around 1470 for the church of Sta. Maria dell'Osservanza in Bologna. The church was demolished and then rebuilt in 1814; however by 1750 the painting had already been acquired by Augustus III of Saxony in Dresden.

ERCOLE DE'ROBERTI
Ferrara ca. 1450—Ferrara 1496
The Agony in the Garden and the Betrayal of Christ, and *Christ on the Road to Calvary*
Oil on panel; each 13¾" x 46½".
Inv. nos. 45 and 46
Together with the *Pietà* in the Walker Art Gallery, Liverpool, these formed the predella of the altarpiece over the high altar of the church of San Giovanni in Monte in Bologna, according to the 1603 edition of Cavazzoni's *Guida*; in 1686 they were recorded by Malvasia as hanging behind the altar and in 1732 they were moved to the sacristy of the same church. According to Luigi Crespi they arrived in Dresden in 1750, bought for Augustus III by Guarienti.

ERCOLE DE' ROBERTI. *The Agony in the Garden and the Betrayal of Christ. Christ on the Road to Calvary.* pp. 28–29

The altarpiece of the Pietà, of which these panels formed the predella, was finished by Lorenzo Costa; it is not known whether the commission was originally for de' Roberti, or why he did not finish it. Discussing the panels, Longhi has noted how much de' Roberti's profound and solemn genius is a reflection of Ferrara, the city in which he was brought up and where his style developed, for his brilliance as an artist cannot be explained by divine inspiration, but rather must be understood as a full and complete expression of the local character and stylistic heritage.

These two scenes from the Passion, set in a gloomy, overcast landscape, cannot be fully appreciated without the panel of the *Pietà* in its original position between them. The group of mourning figures at the right in the second panel is the key to an understanding of the mood of the whole; the different events which unroll in a continuous narrative create a single and monumental heroic exaltation of Christ's Passion. (R.V.)

FRANCIA (FRANCESCO RAIBOLINI). *Adoration of the Magi.*
This painting dates from the period in Francia's career when he was working in Bologna under the influence of Ferrarese artists, notably Ercole de' Roberti and Lor-

FRANCIA (FRANCESCO RAIBOLINI)
Bologna ca. 1450—Bologna 1517
Adoration of the Magi (ca. 1499)
Oil on panel; 16″ x 23″.
Inv. no. 49
First recorded in the Dresden inventories in 1754, when it was attributed to Perugino.

CORREGGIO (ANTONIO ALLEGRI)
Correggio 1489—Correggio 1534
Adoration of the Shepherds, or *Holy Night* (ca. 1530)
Oil on panel; 100¾″ x 74″.
Inv. no. 152
Commissioned in 1522 by Alberto Pratonari for the family chapel in the church of San Prospero, at Reggio Emilia, the painting was transferred in 1640 by Francesco I d'Este to his private gallery; then in 1746, Francesco III sold this and other paintings to August III of Saxony for the Dresden Gallery.

enzo Costa, with whom he had had direct contact.

This work does not reflect any awareness of artistic trends in Rome or of Perugino's style, which was to be so important to him after 1500. Francia's subsequent enthusiasm for Roman styles was to stifle the inventiveness and fertility of his earlier years, encouraging instead a mechanical repetition of borrowed models. Costa's *Adoration of the Magi* in the Brera dates from the same year, and the two artists worked together in Bologna in 1505 on a cycle in the small church of St. Cecilia producing a work which typifies the artistic tastes of their rather provincial society. A comparison with Costa's work, while showing a similarity in the organization of space, is more interesting for the difference it reveals in the approach of the two artists. Francia's arrangement of the figures in the narrative scene is analytically descriptive rather than anecdotal, in contrast with Costa's work; it is worth noting the way in which he raises and isolates the Holy Family and his bold, bravura touches such as the group of youths wearing extravagant hats. Particular motifs, such as the dog, are not added for their incidental charm, but rather are designed to convey a sense of elegance and reflect the exalted status of the three Magi.

The incorporation of classical remains in the painting, which is a frequent characteristic of the art of the time, is representative not only of the discoveries being made all over Italy during the Renaissance, but also of the classical ideals which were being adopted in the creation of a new society. (R.V.)

CORREGGIO (ANTONIO ALLEGRI)
Correggio 1489—Correggio 1534
The Madonna with St. George
Tempera on panel; 112″ x 74¾″.
Inv. no. 153
Executed for the Oratorio di San Pietro Martire at Modena, the painting was acquired in 1649 by Francesco I d'Este; in 1746 Francesco III d'Este ceded it to August III of Saxonv.

CORREGGIO. *Adoration of the Shepherds,* or *Holy Night.*   *p. 31*

The immediate fame which this painting acquired, and still continues to enjoy, was reflected at the time in the persistence of Alfonso II d'Este's attempts to buy it in 1587. It occupied the place of honor in the d'Este family's collection, as Charles de Brosses described in a letter to Monsieur de Neuilly in 1740, noting how the painting was hung in the gallery's last room as a *pièce de résistance* to end one's visit to the collection. The French writer adds, "Forgive me, divine Raphael, if none of your works have so moved me as this one has!" The *Adoration* was one of the main prizes which inspired the negotiations which were to bring the most important works in the d'Este collection into the hands of Augustus III of Saxony in 1746.

It has been noted how Correggio in this work followed the example of Titian's style, particularly of the *Pesaro Altarpiece*, though this is obviously not the sole influence. While certainly aware of Venetian art he was equally open to other styles; his early admiration for Mantegna was tempered by his later appreciation for Emilian artists, particularly Dosso Dossi, which served to bring him to the forefront of contemporary artistic developments. The court of Correggio—where the artist was patronized by the poetess Veronica Gambara, wife of the ruler Gilbert—was refined and sophisticated, in contact with the other Italian courts and on a level with those of the Gonzagas in Mantua and the d'Estes in Ferrara. (R.V.)

CORREGGIO (ANTONIO ALLEGRI). *The Madonna with St. George.*

Correggio's life and career were divided almost exclusively between Parma and Correggio; despite this his style developed continuously and he successfully avoided the dangers of staid repetition or provinciality. He had direct experience of Mantegna's and Parmigianino's works, while he was greatly influenced by the style of the Ferrarese Dosso Dossi; in Rome, which he visited in 1519, he saw the Sistine Chapel and Raphael's Stanze. As a whole he kept abreast of all the most important artistic developments of the century.

The space is constructed on regular, almost academic lines, the figures arranged around a central axis. The landscape background behind the Virgin's shoulders places the scene in a natural setting which harmonizes with the floral decorations and the playful putti. These motifs are not second-hand borrowings from other artists, but features which the artist is able to manipulate to create a scene of great

PARMIGIANINO (FRANCESCO
MAZZOLA)
Parma 1503—Casalmaggiore 1540
*The Madonna in Glory between St. Stephen and
St. John the Baptist* (1539–40)
Oil on panel; 99½" x 63".
Inv. no. 160
Executed for the church of the Sta. Stefano in
Casalmaggiore, the painting was acquired by
Francesco I, Duke of Modena; then along with
the other paintings from the d'Este Collection, it
was sold in 1746 by Francesco III to Augustus
III of Saxony for the Dresden Gallery.

originality, richness and significance. This painting is a particularly good example
of Correggio's creativeness, illustrating how he was able to adopt the pictorial conventions of his time and create something which, rather than being stilted and dull,
is both fertile and imaginative. (R.V.)

PARMIGIANINO (FRANCESCO MAZZOLA). *The Madonna in Glory between
St. Stephen and St. John the Baptist.*

This painting has always enjoyed great fame, so much so that its original owners,
the community of Casalmaggiore, had to refuse numerous offers for it, among
which one of the most pressing was that made by the Duke of Mantua, Ferdinand
Gonzaga. They were, however, unable to refuse a request from their own ruler,
Francesco I d'Este, who had it hung in a place of honor in his gallery in Modena.

The rigid arrangement of the various parts, which establishes a sense of definite
hierarchy between them, avoids the danger of becoming too schematic through the
vibrancy and tension of Parmigianino's style.

Parmigianino was certainly aware of the work of his near contemporary Michelangelo Anselmi, the Emilian artist he was following closely during this period

PARMIGIANINO (FRANCESCO
MAZZOLA)
Parma 1503—Casalmaggiore 1540
Madonna of the Rose (1531)
Oil on panel; 43" x 34¾".
Inv. no. 161
According to Vasari, the painting was originally
intended to represent *Venus with Cupid*; but
Aretino, who had commissioned it, rejected it,
and had the subject changed into a religious
theme. It was then given to Clement VII on the
occasion of the latter's arrival in Bologna for the
coronation of Charles V. After passing to the
Zani collection in Bologna, it was sold in 1752,
through Luigi Crespi, to Augustus III for the
Dresden Gallery.

of activity. While Parmigianino's works have a very definite quality of their own, they grow out of a knowledge of contemporary figurative styles and they can always be seen as part of a particular cultural milieu. Throughout his works one can follow the development of his style in its richness and creative originality. Here the painting is arranged in two planes, divided and yet unified by the balustrade, a technique which can also be found among other artists of the region. (R.V.)

GUERCINO (GIOVANNI FRANCESCO BARBIERI)
Cento, Ferrara 1591—Bologna 1666
The Ecstasy of St. Francis (ca. 1623)
Oil on canvas; 63¾″ x 50″.
Inv. no. 356
The painting appears in the 1698 catalogue of the Ranuzzi collection in Bologna; its authenticity having been established by the Accademia Clementina, it was put up for sale in 1756, and acquired that year by the Dresden Gallery.

PARMIGIANINO (FRANCESCO MAZZOLA). *p. 35*

Together with the *Madonna of the Long Neck* this is one of Parmigianino's best known works, one of those in which he displays the characteristics and tendencies which are fundamental to his style as a whole.

The particular appeal of this painting derives from the fact that the original subject matter is retained in the final version, where Classical and Christian meanings join together. The Madonna is also Venus.

The various elements and references which, though combined in this work, nevertheless retain their individuality, give one of the best and most eloquent examples of Parmigianino's style. In his use of symbols he is drawing from esoteric doctrines and sophisticated culture, understood only by the initiate. The meanings are various and interlinked. The rose without thorns, for example, symbolizes the Immaculate Conception, though in this case the significance might be extended to represent Christ's place of birth. The globe is a formal symbol which, in its circularity, represents the totality of the universe. (R.V.)

GUERCINO. *The Ecstasy of St. Francis*

Guercino is one of the best known and most representative of the seventeenth-century Central Italian school of painters. His contacts with the Carracci, his adoption of their style and techniques, his awareness of developments in Venice and Rome were all part of the essential education of an Emilian artist of his time. He is one of the main protagonists of his field, even if, in present-day opinion, he did not have anything personal or innovative to contribute which might have led to the development of the style; instead he remained up-to-date, sensitively adapting his work to comprehend and co-ordinate different contemporary artistic motifs.

This painting should be seen in relation with the *St. Francis in Ecstasy* in the Louvre, of which it is a variation rather than a new version. The Paris work is dated 1620; this one has generally, and probably rightly, been dated a few years later. St. Benedict's absence leaves an obvious gap in the composition which becomes, as a whole, less dynamic and articulate, tending rather to the simple and the schematic. The large number of copies and variations of the 1620 painting is a reflection of its popularity and of Guercino's success, justifying the reputation that he enjoyed as the most important artist working in Bologna after Guido Reni's death. (R.V.)

DOMENICO FETI. *The Parable of the Lost Coin.* *p. 39*

While Feti was influenced by Elsheimer and Cigoli in Rome, the most important factor in the development of his style was his knowledge of Caravaggio's works. These initial influences were lasting, affecting the way in which he saw Rubens' works in Mantua as well as the paintings of the Venetian school, of which he became fully aware during his late years. By this time the various elements which made up his style could be expressed in a fully unified form. This painting is one of a series of Parables, usually dated between 1618 and 1622, which Feti painted late in life. The series enjoyed considerable success; they were much copied and a number of examples found their way into various European collections, reflecting the

continued popularity of Parable paintings. The Dresden painting was in the collection of Charles I. After his execution it was sold to the Archduke William Leopold, Governor of the Low Countries, from whom it passed to the Imperial collections in Prague and Vienna; and from there it finally moved to Dresden.

There is little of Rubens' influence but the effect of Caravaggio's style is decisive in this painting, where the space is defined through light and shade, which serves to divide the whole into two parts. The bare, grimy poverty of the room—in which the woman is bent double, holding a lamp and looking for her lost coin—the use of free, painterly brush strokes to depict the meagre furnishings, and the bold foreshortening of the fallen stool all reflect the profound influence which Feti's Roman experience had on the development of his style. (R.V.)

DOMENICO FETI
Rome ca. 1589—Venice 1624
The Parable of the Lost Coin (1618–22)
Oil on panel; 21¾″ x 17¼″.
Inv. no. 418
The painting was bought in 1742 by Augustus III for the Dresden collection.

GIUSEPPE MARIA CRESPI. *Confirmation.* p. 40

As an artist Crespi remained tied to the Bolognese school of realism, seldom leaving the city except for an occasional visit to Florence. However, he was able to bring a new impetus to the academic style of the Carracci, without veering towards the dangers of glibness, provinciality or easy popularity. Instead, he gave it a greater versatility, securing for it a place in eighteenth-century European painting. Although the genre subjects he painted may appear to limit him to the particular and the insignificant, it was in fact this conscious preference which did so much to broaden the school he championed in his works.

Marangoni, the first critic to appreciate Crespi's style, described the series of the Seven Sacraments as his greatest work. Through his sensitivity and imagination he steers clear of the pomposity of the Counter Reformation and avoids the standardized treatment which might have been prescribed by a Cardinal Paleotti or Borromeo. It has been noted that in his trips to Tuscany he would have had access, through the Medici Collection, to contemporary European art and in particular to Dutch figurative styles, whose precise vision he interprets in terms of light. In his historically accurate and objective record of Bolognese society he never becomes coldly removed from his subject matter, but rather is constantly and warmly identifying himself with the reality he depicts. (R.V.)

BARTOLOMEO MANFREDI. *The Guardroom.* p. 41

Manfredi followed Caravaggio so closely that many, even among his contemporaries, have confused his works with those of his master. His popularity with northern artists was such that the German Sandrart, writing around about 1630, speaks of a "Manfrediana Methodus" which was adopted by the realistic genre painters who had settled in Italy. Manfredi's own life was lived in the settings which he was able to describe so accurately in his works; as Baglioni wrote, he died young and debauched. He was patronized by Cardinal Barberini. He also worked a great deal in Tuscany, where he painted fairs, feasts, and genre scenes.

This painting, datable to the years between 1615 and 1620, is perhaps the most important in a series of works on unusual themes in which he was constantly varying and rearranging the characters and objects to best bring out the everyday world of tavern life. The *St. Peter's Denial* in the Braunschweig gallery belongs to the same group and has nearly identical measurements.

This large composition is organized like a theatrical scene: the actors seem caught in the moment when the curtain rises. The space is defined by the two lance-carrying soldiers on the left and right. The taste for classical references combined with a taste for profanation is very characteristic of Manfredi's work. The soldiers are playing cards on an antique marble sarcophagus, on whose sides there is a decoration in relief showing a procession of figures in togas approaching a priest.

Manfredi's scene is perhaps taken from life, though its underlying significance seems to imply that the academic style—classicism, order, grace and harmony—will eventually lose in the competition with the painters of reality. (R.V.)

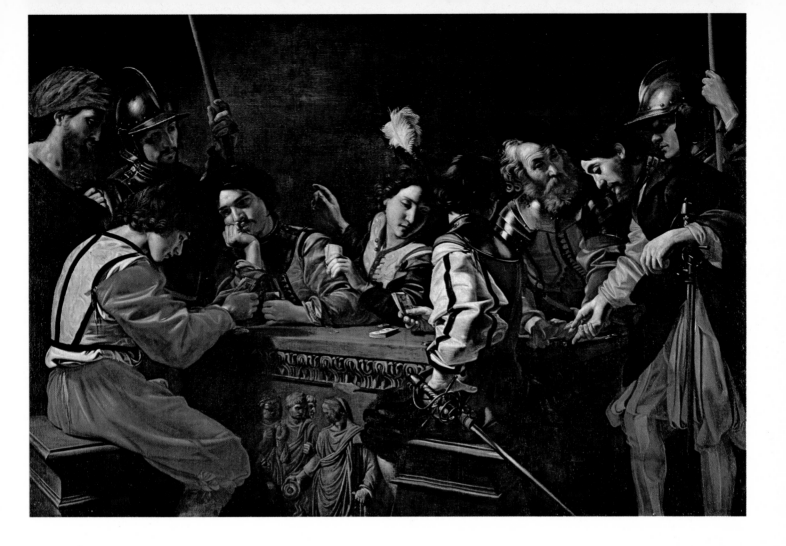

BARTOLOMEO MANFREDI
Ostiano, Mantua ca. 1580—Rome ca. 1620
The Guardroom
Oil on canvas; 67″ x 94½″.
Inv. no. 411
First recorded in the Dresden Gallery in the
1754 inventory, with an attribution to
Caravaggio.

GIUSEPPE MARIA CRESPI
Bologna 1665—Bologna 1747
Confirmation (1712)
Oil on canvas; 49″ x 36½″.
Inv. no. 395
This painting belonged to the series of the Seven
Sacraments commissioned by Cardinal Ottoboni,
a Roman collector. Generally dated around
1712, it was acquired from Ottoboni's heirs for
Augustus III around about 1750.

VALENTIN DE BOULLOGNE. *The Card Players.* p. 42

Valentin, a brother and son of painters, arrived in Rome in 1613, when he discovered the works of Caravaggio and immediately recognized their potential. He abandoned his French associations, and rather than try to enroll in the Academy of San
Luca he joined the school of the "*Bentvogels*" which was favored by the Dutch and
the Germans. With other northern naturalists he became one of Bartolomeo Manfredi's pupils. He developed a style sharply opposed to that of the classicists, as can
be seen in the contrast between his own work and that of Poussin on the walls of St.
Peter's. In his paintings he recreates the world of soldiers, prostitutes and gamblers
in the taverns and brothels he frequented during his short life. He had a reputation
as some sort of Don Juan, and was known as a heavy drinker and smoker; his contemporaries attributed his death to excess and intemperance in life.

He was one of Caravaggio's most important, coherent followers. He enjoyed
great fame, and the fact that he was collected by Cardinal Mazarin and that his
canvases were considered as valuable as Guercino's is significant. His best period,
in the '20s and '30s, came after an initial, and less original, adoption of Caravaggio's style. This work belongs to that period, and can be dated ca. 1624. The theme
derives from a painting by Caravaggio then in the possession of Cardinal Barberini,
where his protegé Valentin would certainly have seen it, though it should be noted
that he was able to make use of it without copying it. The attention is concentrated
on the three characters without the distraction of any superfluous detail; the light
filtering into the darkness picks out the cheat's dry, miserly features, the hat with
the feather, and the rather unhealthy, puffy face of the cheated young man. At the
latter's shoulder is the accomplice, who is included solely for the effect of his raised
hand and his sinister, plotting eyes which oversee the intrigue. It is an audacious
piece of painting carried off with pictorial bravura. There exist other works on the 41

same subject, apart from Caravaggio's, but they in no way take away from this one; one might point to *The Card Players* and *The Game of Cards* by Manfredi.

Valentin died impoverished and was buried at the expense of Cassiano del Pozzo, whose portrait he had painted; beside his name in the register of deaths for the parish of Santa Maria del Popolo is inscribed *"pictor famosus."* (R.V.)

ANDREA MANTEGNA. *Holy Family with Elizabeth and the Infant St. John.*
This is possibly the picture mentioned by Ridolfi in 1648 as being at the Giusti in Venice. Cavalcaselle identified it as perhaps the Madonna painted for the Marchioness of Ferrara in 1485. Paccagnini finally concludes from a letter of 1491 that it might be one of those small paintings given by the Gonzagas to various of their friends. Together with the *Madonna with Angels and Saints* painted for Santa Maria in Organo in Verona (today in Milan Castle), and the *Madonna and Child with Saints* and the *Holy Family* in the National Gallery in London, it represents one of the greatest achievements of the artist's late period—from which the most complex and most successful work is the so-called *Madonna della Vittoria*, today in the Louvre. Paccagnini rightly stresses the importance in these works of a kind of tonal mood which directly anticipates developments in sixteenth-century Venetian painting. We should also note the importance of the composition—entirely free (especially in these small or medium-sized works) of any obsession with perspective, and governed by the perfect modeling and positioning of the figures, which as it were give finite outline to what is solid, abstract geometric space. The vivid, enamel-like texture of the colors, used to define architectonic planes within the restricted area enclosed by the frame and blocked by the direct, fixed looks of the faces, also contributes to this effect. (R.M.)

ANTONELLO DA MESSINA. *St. Sebastian.*   *pp. 44–45*
42   The various identifications and attributions of this great work are extremely hard

VALENTIN DE BOULLOGNE.
Coulommiers-en-Brie 1591—Rome 1632
The Cardplayers (ca. 1624)
Oil on canvas; 37¼″ x 54″.
Inv. no. 408
At one time in the Palazzo Sciarra in Rome, later in the Prague Collection with an attribution to Caravaggio; acquired for the Dresden Gallery in 1749.

ANDREA MANTEGNA
Isola di Carturo 1431—Mantua 1500
Holy Family with Elizabeth and the Infant St. John (1495–1500)
Tempera on panel; 29¾″ x 24¼″.
Inv. no. 51
Acquired in 1876.

Left, detail right
ANTONELLO DA MESSINA
Messina 1430—Messina 1479
St. Sebastian (ca. 1476)
Tempera on wood transferred to canvas;
67⅓" x 33½".
Inv. no. 52
In the inventories of the Arundel Collection until 1654; then passed into the Olmütz collection as a work by Giovanni Bellini. Bought in Vienna by Endris, who sold it to the Dresden Gallery as a work by Bonsignori.

**CIMA DA CONEGLIANO (GIOVANNI
BATTISTA CIMA)**
Conegliano ca. 1460—Conegliano 1517 or 1518
Presentation of the Virgin (ca. 1500)
Oil on panel; 41⅓″ x 57″.
Inv. no. 63
In the Dresden Gallery since 1743. Acquired
from an unidentified Venetian church.

46

GIORGIONE and TITIAN
Castelfranco ca. 1477—Venice 1510; Pieve di
Cadore ca. 1488–90—Venice 1576
Sleeping Venus
Oil on canvas; 42½" x 69".
Inv. no. 185
Bought from the dealer Le Roy in 1697. This
was the Venus painted for Gerolamo Marcello.

to follow. Quite apart from the old attributions to "Giambellino" and Bonsignori, it was ascribed by Gluck to Lotto, and by Morelli, more reasonably, to Pietro da Messina.

Cavalcaselle's attribution has now, except for Morelli's initial doubts and the suggestion of Gluck's, become the generally accepted one. Originally it was most probably the left-hand leaf of a *pala* (altarpiece) which Sansovino tells us existed in the church of San Giuliano in Venice. In the middle was a wooden statue of *St. Roch*, and then a *St. Christopher* to balance the *St. Sebastian*. Sansovino attributed the *St. Christopher* to Antonello and the *St. Sebastian* to Pino da Messina (Jacobello or Jacopino, Antonello's son), but this was probably just a slip. Furthermore the Arundel Collection, where the work was until the mid-seventeenth century, also possessed a wooden *St. Roch* of Venetian origin, possibly the center of this triptych.

In the background a precise Mantegnesque reference to the architectural details of the *Martyrdom of St. Christopher* in the Eremitani represents a kind of intellectual homage to Antonello's great colleague—with whom, however, he quite distinctly differs, especially in this superb work, in which the monumental scale of the foreground acts as an anchor to the enormous serenity of the background perspective. Though full of rich Venetian "light," it is reminiscent of the young Piero della Francesca. Longhi has pointed out that the first idea for the painting came from a drawing at the Albertina in Vienna, showing the saint in profile. (R.M.)

CIMA DA CONEGLIANO (GIOVANNI BATTISTA CIMA). *Presentation of the Virgin.*
The most obvious characteristic of this extraordinary work of Cima's is its narrative structural style, which establishes a clear relationship with that of Carpaccio. Specialist criticism has been much concerned with this relationship; but from Fry, through Fiocco, to Coletti, there has been little agreement over the thematic and stylistic "precedence" between the two painters. Coletti would appear to be right in seeing this panel, together with the Berlin *Miracle of St. Mark* and the Birmingham *Crucifixion*, as the clearest products of some kind of contact between them. In Cima's work the sheer exuberance of the architectural "scenery," with its magnificent, minutely detailed, elegant "Lombardy-style" polychrome marbles, of the play of architectural harmonies, and of the limpid light in which the whole work is bathed, has a deliciously "temporary" feel to it, which is lacking in the visionary rationality of Carpaccio's scenes. At the same time the relationship between the figures and the architectural features—which is integrated in Carpaccio—because of the precise, but fragmented way in which they are observed in Cima's work, is often rather clumsy. The painting can be dated to the same years as the *Sacred Conversation* in Berlin and the Accademia di Venezia painted for the Carità. (R.M.)

GIORGIONE and TITIAN. *Sleeping Venus.*   *pp. 48-49*
Strangely enough, having entered the Saxony collection as a Giorgione, this famous work was then classified as a Titian, and then finally, in a catalogue in 1835, attributed to an anonymous Venetian painter. It was Morelli (1886) who re-ascribed it to Giorgione and identified it as the canvas painted for the Casa Marcello, as recorded by Michiel: "The canvas of the nude Venus asleep in a landscape with Cupid was by Zorzo da Castelfranco, though the landscape and the Cupid were finished by Titian." The Cupid in question is in fact there, underneath the restoration done on the painting in 1843 by Schirmer, who had established its existence beneath previous restoration work, but left it hidden because of the picture's poor state of preservation. The absence of this Cupid is one of the arguments always used by those who maintain that the painting is by Titian. From Hourticq (1930) to the less convinced

47

Bonicatti (1964) it has been claimed that Titian's hand is clearly traceable in the overall harmony of the work—in the marvelous section of landscape, so perfectly integrated with the mood of the picture as a whole. We agree with Pignatti that, unless Titian deliberately painted the landscape in a Giorgionesque style to fit in with the rest of the picture, a thorough cleaning off of the heavy layers of varnish, restoration work, and covering coats of paint, would make the differences evident. Again according to Pignatti this Venus dates from immediately after Giorgione's decoration of the Fondaco dei Tedeschi, and "initiates Giorgione's mature phase, in which he was conscious above all of the tonal relationships between figure and landscape." And indeed this "unity," despite the problem of collaboration, is precisely what makes the work so outstanding, deriving its strength from the reclining figure, which gives coherent meaning to both the landscape and the picture as a whole—and if in the figures on the Fondaco meaningful unity had posed a problem, here the supreme solution has been found. (R.M.)

TITIAN
Pieve di Cadore ca. 1488–90—Venice 1576
Portrait of a Young Woman with a Fan (Lavinia as a Bride)
Oil on canvas; 40″ x 33¾″.
Inv. no. 170
Part of the d'Este collection purchased by King Augustus III in 1746.

TITIAN. *Portrait of a Young Woman with Fan (Lavinia as a Bride).*
Critics have from the outset been unable to agree over whether this is a portrait of the young Lavinia, or more vaguely, as Scannelli claimed, a mistress of the painter.

A copy by Rubens (Vienna) and a drawing by van Dyck (Chatsworth) testify to the picture's well-deserved fame—due in no small part to the curious, intimate pose of the girl, with the interplay between the fan and the subtly beckoning look in her eyes. This domestic mood also comes from the luminous effects of the white dress against the warm texture of the background. The picture is an anomaly among Titian's portraits: indeed it constitutes a sort of interim of intense serenity, which yet does not detract from the subtle psychological ambiguity of the girl's distinctive pose. (R.M.)

TITIAN. *Portrait of a Painter with Palm Leaf.*   *p. 52*
Apart from the assertion by Tscheuschner—who mistook the painter's box for that of a surgeon—that this masterly painting is of some saintly doctor (martyred as indicated by the palm), common opinion subscribes to Cook's suggestion that it is a portrait of Antonio Palma, nephew of Palma the Elder and father of Palma the Younger.

The three-quarter length (starting from knee level), and the angle of the pose, place this masterpiece among that group of portraits painted around the same year, which include the *Man with a Clock* in Copenhagen and the *Man with a Flute* in Detroit.

The splendid rhythm conveyed by the subject's stance is here set in marvelous relief by the landscape on the left, cut off by the balustrade with the "still-life" of the painter's equipment on it. The sunset light brings infinitely subtle variations of tone into overall harmony. (R.M.)

TITIAN. *The Tribute Money.*   *p. 53*
Vasari mentions this magnificent work as having been painted for the door of an armoire in Alfonso I d'Este's studio. It is clear, both from the cramped impression the picture gives, and from a copy in the Accademia di San Luca in Rome, that the canvas has been cut away on the sides.

Gronau (1904) correctly grouped this picture together with the *Madonna and Child with Four Saints* which is also in Dresden, the *Madonna of the Cherries* in Vienna, and the *Annunciation* in Treviso; but he was probably out by a few years in dating it between 1512 and 1515. The superb composition achieves a sense of harmony through the contrast of attitude between the two figures (unfortunately weakened by the mutilation), rather than through the violent tensions of light and "expressiveness" which were to appear a few years later in the Vienna *Bravo.* The

TITIAN
Pieve di Cadore ca. 1488–90—Venice 1576
Portrait of a Painter with a Palm Leaf (1561)
Oil on canvas; 54¼" x 45½".
Signed and dated: MDLXI/ANNO . . .
NATUS/AETATIS
SUAE XLVI/TITIANUS PICTOR
ET/AEQUES CAESARIS
Inv. no. 172
From the Casa Marcello in Venice.

intense, inward quality of the meaningful space in this "portrait" of Christ at the same time creates a strong, harmonious focal point for the exquisite economy of movement.

In the prophetic, mystical "inner life" of this Christ there is a close similarity with other, contemporary masterpieces by Titian, such as the Ickworth *Gentleman*, the *Young Man in a Red Cap* in the Frick Collection, New York, and the *Portrait of a Young Man* in Frankfurt. (R.M.)

LEANDRO BASSANO *Moses Striking the Rock for Water.*   *p. 54*
Berenson attributed this canvas to Jacopo Bassano, although this is difficult to maintain in the light of Arslan's studies on the early work of Leandro, of which it is most probably a part. The peculiar timbre of the tense color is such as to tone down and restrain any chiaroscuro effects: color and composition are incorporated to form a unified tapestry of figures, landscape and sky. From this characteristic style comes the effect, noted by Arslan, by which the trees seem to have been printed onto the tense backdrop of the sky.

These stylistic elements date the work to before 1582, the year in which Leandro completed the altarpiece of the *Circumcision* for the parish church at Rosa, a

TITIAN
Pieve di Cadore ca. 1488–90—Venice 1576
The Tribute Money (ca. 1516–18)
Oil on canvas; 29½" x 22".
Inscribed "Ticianus F."
Inv. no. 169
Bought by King Augustus III of Saxony from the d'Este Collection in 1746.

work which marks the end of his early development and the beginning of his mature style. In this interesting group of early works—of which *The Departure for Canaan* is particularly close in style to the Dresden work—the *Moses* is perhaps the most complex and impressive. (R.M.)

LEANDRO BASSANO
Bassano 1557—Bassano 1623
Moses Striking the Rock for Water
Oil on canvas; 72¼." x 119¼.".
Inv. no. 253
From the Grimaldi collection in Venice, first appearing in the Dresden inventory in 1747.

PALMA THE ELDER (JACOPO NEGRETTI). *Jacob and Rachel*   *p. 55*
The attribution of this work to Giorgione is very old. It would appear, indeed, that its first owners, the Venetian Malipiero family, claimed it was by him; and it was recorded as such in the gallery inventory before 1753.

At the end of the nineteenth century conflicting opinions began to be voiced. It was attributed to Cariani by Cavalcaselle; then finally to Palma the Elder by Hirt and Morelli. Everything indeed points to a date posterior to 1520.

It is one of the finest of the painter's late works, and in it he seems to return to the "arcadian," elegiac, subtly emotional, anecdotal style of his youth.

The embrace of the two protagonists at the center of a wide landscape is isolated in a small, but intense arc of feeling. The "minor" details of the narrative are developed through subtle suggestion and in perfect harmony of emotional mood, the

PALMA THE ELDER (JACOPO NEGRETTI)
Serina, Bergamo ca. 1480—Venice 1528
Jacob and Rachel (after 1525)
Oil on canvas; 57½" x 98½".
Inv. no. 192
From the Casa Malipiero. Listed in the 1753
inventory as being by Giorgione.

marvelous series of smaller figures framed in patches of green creating a sort of exact counterpoint to the central visual theme.

Mariacher, who dates the painting after 1525, correctly discerned in these apparently secondary details a new taste for the popular, which seems to anticipate the rustic scenes of the Bassanos. (R.M.)

PAOLO VERONESE. *The Marriage Feast at Cana.*   *pp. 56-57*

A discussion about the original location of this work and other problems concerning the four Palazzo Cuccina canvases now in Dresden is contained in the text for *The Cuccina Family Presented to the Virgin* (p. 58–59). In the case of *The Marriage Feast,* Veronese criticism has been mainly concerned with the extent of the collaboration of assistants, and the identification of their number and contributions. Pallucchini (1963), for example, maintains that the figure of the Madonna is by Benedetto, while more recently Pignatti (1976) limits the contribution of the school to the less important parts. It will be remembered that in 1934 Fiocco identified the figure in the foreground proposing a toast as a self-portrait by Veronese; a comparison with the self-portrait in the Louvre *Marriage Feast*—the figure of the violinist—makes this theory very improbable.

A very interesting preparatory drawing exists for this work (which is dated between 1565 and 1570), and is now preserved in the Kupferstichkabinett in Berlin. It is a study of the composition and arrangement of the principal groups around the table, which contains various differences from the final version. There is a higher vanishing point, and instead of the central, slightly leaning figure of the cup-bearer—which serves to divide the composition into two components—there is a male figure with bent shoulders and a twisted pose, creating an impression of free dyna-

mism. The replacement of that concentrated figure by the far more relaxed one of
the cup-bearer in the final painting, although they both fulfill the same dividing
role in the composition, loosens the driving tension of the sketch, which would
have seemed out of place in relation to the three other calmer works in the cycle.
(R.M.)

PAOLO VERONESE. *Presentation of the Cuccina Family to the Virgin. pp. 58–59*
Veronese painted this enormous canvas, together with three other works—*The*

PAOLO VERONESE (PAOLO CALIARI)
Verona 1528—Venice 1588
The Marriage Feast at Cana
Oil on canvas; 81¾″ x 180½″.
Inv. no. 226
Painted for the Palazzo Cuccina in Venice;
bought in 1645 by Francesco I d'Este; then in
1746 by King Augustus III, Elector of Saxony.

Road to Calvary, The Adoration of the Shepherds, and *The Marriage Feast at Cana*—for the Palazzo Cuccina (now Papadopoli) at Sant'Aponal on the Grand Canal. All four—which passed as a unit into the d'Este collection, and then into that of Frederick Augustus II—were intended for one room, although it is not clear which, in the present state of the Palazzo. But given the dimensions of the canvases, each wall must have been well over fifteen feet long.

Critics agree, given the exact differences and movement of the respective viewpoints, that this *Presentation* would have hung opposite *The Road to Calvary*. The members of the family shown in the painting still have not been definitely identi-

57

fied, nor has the work been precisely dated, as attribution of a date would depend on the dates of birth or death of those depicted. Nevertheless various suggestions have been advanced—somewhat arbitrarily, in view of the impossibility of identification.

It now seems certain, however, that it dates from around 1565, the same period in which Veronese painted *The Family of Darius* (in the National Gallery in London), a work stylistically related to this in several respects. The marvelous composition, set entirely in the foreground, and weighted heavily to the left, gives the scene a kind of theatricality, without in any way disturbing the overall balance. The family palazzo appears in the background. The members of the family being presented to the Virgin by Faith and Charity appear in either ceremonial or direct, natural, "narrative" poses. All the brushwork is extremely fluid, often creating realistic impasto effects enhanced by rich, vibrant white touches of light.

Every part of the painting is of the same exceptional quality—a fact which in itself dates the work from before 1570, when Veronese began to employ helpers on a massive scale, as can be seen, for example, in *The Road to Calvary*. (R.M.)

Above; detail right
PAOLO VERONESE (PAOLO CALIARI)
Verona 1528—Venice 1588
Presentation of the Cuccina Family to the Virgin
(after 1565)
Oil on canvas; 65¾" x 163¾".
Inv. no. 224
Painted for the Palazzo Cuccina; bought in 1645 by Francesco I d'Este; then in 1746 by King Augustus III, Elector of Saxony.

TINTORETTO (JACOPO ROBUSTI). *The Liberation of Arsinoë*.   *p. 60*
Lucan tells how Arsinoë, sister of Cleopatra, fled from Alexandria with the help of Ganymede.

Apart from Pittaluga, who holds that the work could belong to Tintoretto's late maturity (after 1570), all other critics are agreed that it dates from around 1550–53.

This canvas is striking in the way it centers on the flexible, sinuous coordination of the two main figures. Resuming the splendid synopsis of the female in the *Leda* (formerly in the Contini Bonacossi collection), the composition possesses the extraordinary rhythm found in some of the *Bible Story* paintings done in Madrid for Philip II, notably in the billowing, intertwining movement of *Esther and Ahasuerus*.

In the balanced, decisive cadence of the boat in the immediate foreground we feel the subtle, but insinuating vein of sensuality emanating from the sumptuous colors of Tintoretto's palette in his marvelous depiction of "nature" during these years from the waning, almost spent opulence of summer landscapes, to the exqui-

site freedom of his nudes. In the dynamic, enveloping curve of the boat, the clearly-defined sickle shape sets up a precise equilibrium that, by reaction, can evoke an intense, visionary state of feeling. (R.M.)

TINTORETTO (JACOPO ROBUSTI). *The Archangel Michael.*

Admirable as this painting is, critics have not always been able to agree about its place in the artist's oeuvre. Berenson, for instance, attributed it to the school of Tintoretto; while Loeser identified it as one of the scenes of the Apocalypse painted by Palma Giovane for the Scuola di San Giovanni Evangelista in Venice.

Although we would perhaps concede that the studio had a hand in it, it is in our opinion one of the most lofty conceptions of Tintoretto's old age—which in itself already presents very special problems, somewhat neglected by critics so far.

We would in fact agree with Pallucchini in seeing in this last period of the painter's career a kind of deepening of the narrative tendency in his work, so that it seems to absorb and outshine some of the elements of the grand, spectacular language which characterizes his entire development. On the other hand works such as this, and above all masterpieces like the *Birth of the Virgin* in Mantua or *The Last Supper* in San Giorgio in Venice, show how powerful still, and in a sense how much more complex is his ability to create subtle and spectacular patterns, brought often into sharp relief by daring, dramatic movement and visionary effects of light.

The structural strength of this *Archangel Michael* derives essentially from the ingenious device of identifying the Archangel's spear setting the fiends of hell to rout as one of the axes of the St. Andrew's cross that subtends the whole composition. Besides this quite distinctive division there is also that of the two worlds, Heaven and Hell, each enacting its own drama, each brought to life by the rich, supremely expressive coloring of Tintoretto's last glorious years. (R.M.)

60

TINTORETTO (JACOPO ROBUSTI)
Venice 1518—Venice 1594
The Liberation of Arsinoë (ca. 1550–53)
Oil on canvas; 60¼" x 98¾".
Inv. no. 269
Bought as part of the d'Este collection by King Augustus III in 1746.

TINTORETTO (JACOPO ROBUSTI)
Venice 1518—Venice 1594
The Archangel Michael (1592)
Oil on canvas; 125¼" x 86⅓".
Inv. no. 266
Listed in the 1754 inventory of Augustus III's collection.

BERNARDO STROZZI
Genoa 1581–Venice 1644
Woman with a Bass Viol (ca. 1635)
Oil on canvas; 48″ x 39″.
Inv. no. 658
According to Ratti, originally in the Casa Sagredo, Venice, whence Algarotti took it to Augustus III in 1743.

BERNARDO STROZZI. *Woman with a Bass Viol.*

Lazareff rightly assigned this work to the first phase of Strozzi's Venetian period, giving as his reasons for doing so the strong "Genoese" elements obvious in every aspect of it. These Genoese elements are extremely complex, given the cultural interweavings in Genoa in the previous few decades: the idiom of van Dyck and Rubens predominating, yet at the same time combining with an interest in Barocci, the Sienese "manner," and above all the grand, compelling Lombardy "manner," among which there were close contacts and numerous exchanges. Arriving in Venice in 1630, Strozzi did not substantially alter this complex cultural mold during his last active years, although his handling of color became both stronger and more subtle. This change is vividly apparent here (it should be remembered that musical subjects were a particular favorite with Strozzi), as also in the Malta *Portrait of a Lady* and the *Salome* in Padua. Note the particular care taken over the intense expressiveness of the face, which is the major emotional attraction of the whole picture. (R.M)

63

CANALETTO. *Campo San Giacometto in Rialto.*
This view of San Giacometto was originally a pendent to the *View of the Piazza San Marco towards the Basilica*, which was lost during the Second World War. Criticism is generally agreed in shifting the date of this masterpiece a little towards 1730. It is worth noting the drawing of the same view in the Seilern Collection in London, signed by Canaletto and for a long time held to be a preparatory study for this work, though Constable's suggestion (1962) that it followed from or was copied from the painting seems more likely. Canaletto's early style, with its sense of visual solidity and impenetrable compactness which serve to create an appearance of depth and reality, acquires in this work a very finely balanced sensitivity, expressed in the suffused tension of the color range and the liquid vibrancy of the atmosphere and lighting. The work remains as a testimony to the most lyrical and visionary traditions of the glorious Venetian civilization. **(R.M.)**

CANALETTO (GIOVANNI ANTONIO
CANAL)
Venice 1697—Venice 1768
Campo San Giacometto in Rialto
Oil on canvas; 37½" x 46".
Inv. no. 583
First appeared in Dresden in the 1794 inventory.

CANALETTO. *Piazza San Giovanni e Paolo, Venice.*   *p. 66*
Marchesini mentions this painting in a letter to Stefano Conti dated April 18th, 1725. Between this picture and that of the same subject (today in Montreal) painted for Conti there are several changes of perspective, notably in the viewpoint, so that the respective sizes of the Ospedale and the church differ. These alterations are very probably due also to different positioning of the *camera ottica* which, as is well known, Canaletto used in order to record scenes exactly as they appeared in reality. Painted a few years after his return from Rome, after he had freed himself of the strict illusionistic perspective discipline his father had taught him (his father Bernardo was a well-known scenery painter, which was how he too started), this picture is one of his first masterpieces. Together with the four canvases painted for Conti, the series today at Windsor, and one or two other works, it saw the beginning of his pictorial revolution. This picture from life becomes as it were the most perfect, precisely defined vital field of vision in which separate elements—perspective, the structured composition of masses, the defining power of light—go to cre-

ate a sort of tense, emotional, optical vision which, even where it is merely "sketched," never falls into fashionable, mechanical illustration. The same color tonalities found here, based on almost mathematically calculated "true" variations of light, become integrated in a style which lends sudden new importance to Venice at the moment of its decline.(R.M.)

BERNARDO BELLOTTO. *View of Dresden from the Right Bank of the Elbe.*
This view of Dresden differs from the rest of the Royal Series in the breadth of the scene it embraces—the Augustus bridge from the right bank of the Elbe, observed from above the central, flowing bed of the river. Obviously because of its "pan-

CANALETTO (GIOVANNI ANTONIO CANAL)
Venice 1697—Venice 1768
Piazza San Giovanni e Paolo, Venice (ca. 1725–26)
Oil on canvas; 49¼" x 65".
Inv. no. 582
Acquired through the ambassador Cesareo at the Fiera di San Rocco exhibition in 1725.

BERNARDO BELLOTTO
Venice 1720—Warsaw 1780
View of Dresden from the Right Bank of the Elbe
Oil on canvas; 52½" x 93¼".
Signed and dated below, center: "Bernardo
Bellotto detto Canaletto F. an⁰. 1748".
Inv. no. 606
Given to the Dresden Gallery in 1750.

oramic" nature, the work has much greater luminosity than others in the series; and although still within the tight, abstract quality of Bellotto's style (as opposed to the visual-emotional intensity of the contemporary works of his uncle Canaletto), this creates a remarkable impression of three-dimensional depth. At the same time, in contrast to this coloristic structural abstraction, it should be noted that the "sketched" figures in these pictures by Bellotto are more fully realized than those of his uncle; they stand out and are less stylized, in a manner which ultimately becomes a decisive factor in the views of the so-called Polish period. (R.M)

BERNARDO BELLOTTO. *The Neumarkt in Dresden.*   *p. 68*
The details of Bellotto's move from Venice to Dresden are well known, and to what degree this drastic decision was based on the hitherto unbearable relations with his uncle Antonio Canal—a man of a very difficult character, not lacking in feelings of resentment and envy. Indeed in 1753 Guarienti wrote that Bellotto "having thus acquired a certain reputation annoyed his uncle, who drove him away." That same year (1747) Canaletto himself left for London. Although one should not exaggerate this incompatibility between uncle and nephew, it is nonetheless impossible to explain Bellotto's permanent self-exile from his native city simply by the invitation of the Elector of Saxony, later to become King of Poland as Frederick Augustus II. Bellotto moved with wife and children to Dresden, becoming court painter in 1748. After ten years there, by which time the Seven Years' War had ended, he moved to Vienna. This *Neumarkt* is part of the magnificent Royal Series, which he repeated on a smaller scale for other noble patrons, but also in the original dimensions for the powerful minister Brühl. It is one of the masterpieces of the series. The extraor-

dinary breadth of scale of the scene is set off in the background by the mass of the Frauenkirche, a focal point for the visual scope and tension of the picture, which appears blocked out by a sort of abstract hyper-luminosity. This new "scenic" space invented by Bellotto in the splendid views of his Dresden series, is one of the loftiest, most original, and most important developments in the whole of eighteenth-century painting. (R.M.)

BERNARDO BELLOTTO
Venice 1720—Warsaw 1780
The Neumarkt in Dresden
Oil on canvas; 53″ x 93″.
Inv. no. 610
Painted for the King Augustus III of Saxony, and given to the Gallery in 1750.

ROSALBA CARRIERA. *The Countess of Orzelska.*
Frederick Augustus II's, and later his son's admiration for Rosalba Carriera led to one of the most notable examples of eighteenth-century collecting. The two monarchs in fact succeeded in bringing together some one hundred and fifty-seven pastels by the Venetian painter in their collection in Dresden, most of which fortunately remain intact and constitute the larger part of her oeuvre. Unfortunately many are ignored in studies on the artist, making it difficult—unless one can refer to particular journeys, diaries, or other documentary evidence—to establish a reliable chronology for most of her work.

This portrait of *The Countess of Holstein, née Orzelska* may have been executed either in 1728 during the artist's visit to Gorizia at the time of Charles VI's visit

ROSALBA CARRIERA
Venice 1675—Venice 1757
The Countess of Orzelska
Pastel; 25¼″ x 20″.
Inv. no. 125

GIOVANNI BATTISTA PIAZZETTA
Venice 1683—Venice 1754
Boy Holding a Banner
Oil on canvas; 34¼″ x 28″.
Inv. no. 571
Acquired in 1743 through Count Algarotti.

there, together with portraits of other leading figures at that court, or in 1730 when she went to the court of Vienna itself, though only staying there from May until mid-October.

It is not known when this portrait came into the Elector's collection. It was most probably found in the artist's studio, and bought by Frederick Christian at the time of the latter's last meeting with Carriera in 1739. At this time he acquired a selection of forty works, among which there were some portraits of the Viennese court which Carriera had completed at her leisure in Venice.

This picture provides one of the most exquisite examples of Carriera's mature portrait style, notable for the subtle sensitivity with which the psychological character of the sitter is conveyed. (R.M.)

GIOVANNI BATTISTA PIAZZETTA. *Boy Holding a Banner.*

This is one of the artist's most intense and happiest works, even though its unquestioned greatness retains the influence of Longhi's genre style. However, although elsewhere this might lead to an exaggerated concentration on academic composition and pose, and a heaviness of coloring which may well impair the result and reflect too great a reliance on standard models, in the case of this flag-bearer one must recognize the perfect balance which exists between the soft modelling of the figure and the handling of the shadowy light, which seems to glow from within the materials themselves in bringing out the various forms. In this accomplished handling it differs markedly from some of the artist's other works where the light is used in a very limited and merely descriptive manner. It reflects—as do other works of about 1725, the now generally accepted date of the work—the Bolognese influence of Crespi, applied to the tradition of Venetian portraiture. As a result the pose and all the techniques of lighting, color and tones are used to create an image of powerful psychological insight and immediacy, which tends to be a little disquieting. (R.M)

GIOVANNI BATTISTA TIEPOLO. *The Vision of St. Anne.*

p. 72

Despite the signature and date on this work, critical opinion as to the extent of Giambattista's contribution to the whole is divided. As early as 1896, in the Tiepolo exhibition at Venice, it was not included among those works considered to be indisputably autograph; and it is still generally maintained that Domenico's collaboration could have been important. Many of these doubts are due to the comparison between the finished work and the oil-sketch for it, which is preserved in the Rijksmuseum in Amsterdam. That study preserves a freshness of conception and execution which is lacking in the finished work, partly because of its size and partly because of the visual restrictions where it was originally installed. Apart from this, however, the light, airy setting as well as the fine control of passages and color tones reflect the undoubted intervention of Giambattista. His genius is reflected in the fixed, graduated arrangement of the rising figures, their lightness and mobility preserved through the clear contrasts of the color. The grandiose "mechanics" which are absent from the sketch are part of the spatial emphasis which must be seen as an essential component of this Tiepolesque work. (R.M.)

GIOVANNI BATTISTA TIEPOLO
Venice 1696—Madrid 1770
The Vision of St. Anne
Oil on panel; 96¼″ x 47¼″.
Signed and dated: GIO BATTA TIEPOLO O.
1759
Inv. no. 580A
Executed for the Benedictine monastery of St.
Chiara, in Cividale del Friuli, where it remained
until 1820.

FLEMISH AND BELGIAN PAINTING
15th-20th Centuries

JAN VAN EYCK. *Virgin and Child Enthroned in a Church.*

The frame is original and serves as a bridge from the exterior to the interior of the picture. The patron's coat of arms is probably that of the Giustiniani family at Genoa. At the bottom of the center panel are a date and signature: *"Johannes de Eyck me fecit et co(m)plevit Anno Domini M CCCC XXXVII."* This date was only discovered in 1958; it indicates that the picture is one of van Eyck's very late works, a fact which amazed a number of scholars who were convinced that it was painted several years earlier. Indeed some of them continued to suggest (erroneously!) that it was the work of an earlier period which was simply completed, as the inscription in fact says, a few years before the artist's death.

It is a small and exquisite painting, hardly larger than a precious miniature, yet in these three panels is projected a grandiose architectural setting: a splendid Romanesque church with nave and side aisles. This imposing interior is enlivened with statues, pinnacles, intrically carved capitals, together with floral, plant, spiraling, star and scroll decorative forms profusely distributed on the structural elements, the baldachin, the stained-glass windows, the carpet and the inlaid floor—a wonderful mass of living colors bathed in a soft golden light.

All this is in sharp contrast to the simplicity of the Annunciation scene on the exterior faces of the two doors, in which the monochromatic figures of the Virgin and the Angel Gabriel stand out like ivory statues against the bare space around them. Yet the shadows they cast (the emblem of the dove hovering in the center above Mary is particularly significant) manage to create a feeling of space just as impressive as that of the more complex interior scene shown here.

In this there is a strong sense of perspective created by the lines of the carpet and the rows of capitals and architraves converging towards the central pyramidal

JAN VAN EYCK
Maastricht c. 1390—Bruges 1441
Triptych: Virgin and Child Enthroned in a Church; left wing, *The Archangel Michael with Kneeling Donor*; right wing, *St. Catherine*.
Oil on panel; central panel 13″ x 10¾″.
Side panels 13″ x 5⅛″ (measurements include the original frame).
Signed and dated on the molding of the central panel: *Johannes D^e eyck me fecit et complevit Anno DMM'CCCC'XXXVII' als ixh xan.*
Inv. no. 799

JOOS VAN CLEVE THE ELDER (JOOS VAN DER BEKE)
Cleves or Antwerp c. 1485—Antwerp 1540 or 1541
Adoration of the Magi (ca. 1526–28)
Oil on panel; 98¾" x 72¼".
Inv. no. 809A

mass of the Virgin, which rises from the base of her red mantle to her youthful absorbed face. The sense of perspective is heightened by the receding space of the lateral aisle openings in the side panels, where two saints, magnificent in their youth and beauty, stand in the foreground, related in their proportions, attitudes and meaning not to their surroundings but to the distant figure of the Virgin, who sits with the Child at the further end of the nave, gentle yet somehow dominant: the central and most important figure in the whole composition. (L.C.R.)

JOOS VAN CLEVE. *Adoration of the Magi.*

This large painting was commissioned in 1520 for a church in Genoa. In it we find almost all the basic elements of van Cleve's artistic idiom: the inspiration he draws from Italian models of the early fifteenth century (particularly evident in the figures of Mary and the Child) is miraculously fused with elements developed directly from the Flemish tradition.

In the foreground, the sumptuously dressed figures—every fold of whose clothing has been painted with loving care—the architectural structures with exquisitely rendered carving and reliefs, together with the plant forms in the immediate foreground, which add a further delicately expressive element to the whole picture, are all against a vast and varied landscape background, which stretches away toward the peaceful silence of hills and distant houses, contrasting with the crowd of people, animals and objects in the foreground. Strangely enough this assemblage is not in the least confused or chaotic; each of the central figures is most carefully positioned and there is great economy in the artist's depiction of the mass of detail: the two Evangelists at either side, the foreign kings, the climbing vine of ivy, the marble carvings, the crumbling walls, the glittering stones. Finally, in the group of inquisitive bystanders at the far left of the picture, stands the artist, looking on impassively over the shoulder of Gaspar in the big hat at the rich and magical scene he himself has created. (L.C.R.)

PIETER PAUL RUBENS. *The Boar Hunt.* *pp. 78–79*

It should be noted that some critics propose that this and a group of other similar hunting scenes (in Munich, Marseilles, and New York) are the work of Frans Snyders, an artist who worked with Rubens and was certainly famous in his own day. All these works can be dated around 1618–20 during the years in which Rubens created many of his most dynamic works, giving full rein to his descriptive powers.

In this and other hunting scenes (and in the landscapes now in Vienna and Madrid) Rubens succeeded in investing the natural surroundings with the same dramatic impetus which he gives to his human figures. Nature becomes a protagonist in the drama, but men and animals still have an equally important part to play. This technique is unlike that in the work of modern landscape painters, where the human figure is often merely a mute, inert addition to the scene. It has been said that this cohesion he achieves between the figures and their surroundings makes Rubens the true successor to Brueghel, of whom he was indeed an ardent admirer and collector of his works.

In the middle of this painting there is a mass of men, wild animals and giant roots surrounded by the silent stillness of great leafy trees. The painting literally explodes in the center, in a swirling confusion of bodies, arms, legs, faces, sticks and snouts. There is a tangle of roots and grasses in the foreground, while on the right are dashing horsemen, yet another element in the drama. The thick gloom and luxuriance of the forest press all around, each tree a recognizable individual entity. In the distance on the right a silent, deserted, sunlit glade contrasts strongly with the tumult in the foreground, perhaps as a reminder of how quiet and solemn nature can be when undisturbed by any human presence. (L.C.R.)

PIETER PAUL RUBENS
Siegen, Westphalia 1577—Antwerp 1640
*Bathsheba at the Fountain, Receiving David's
Letter* (ca. 1635)
Oil on panel; 68⅞" x 49⅝".
Inv. no. 965

PIETER PAUL RUBENS. *Bathsheba at the Fountain, Receiving David's Letter.*
The biblical episode was here used largely as a pretext for painting a splendid nude.
The figure is depicted against a magnificent architectural background and attended
by devoted servants. The biblical account is translated into an episode of contemporary life; it seems as though a door has suddenly been opened, affording a glimpse
of something which until now has been carefully hidden from view. This striking
feeling of violating a somehow forbidden privacy has led many critics to speak of
"improvisation," a term which related more to the reaction of the onlooker, and
certainly not that of the painter who—as in all his best paintings—has employed
the most precise planning. The composition is bound together and controlled in a

PIETER PAUL RUBENS
Siegen, Westphalia 1577—Antwerp 1640
Diana Returning from the Hunt (ca. 1615–1617)
Oil on panel; 53½″ x 71⅛″.
Inv. no. 962A

series of contrasting angles and diagonals which spiral towards the focal point of the painting: the firm young body of Bathsheba, the red velvets, the soft furs, the golden hair.

This picture can be dated around 1635, therefore a product of that famous "impetuous brush" of Rubens' late, most happy years. It is filled with nostalgic and affectionate echoes of the great school of Venetian painting which he had loved in his youth: the luminous Veronesian structure, the little black boy against the light, and above all the figure of Bathsheba herself, which was most probably inspired by the seated nymph in Titian's *Diana and Actaeon* (now in Bridgewater house in London, but seen by Rubens while still in the royal collection in Madrid). (L.C.R.)

PIETER PAUL RUBENS. *Diana Returning from the Hunt.* *p. 81*

Dating from about 1615–16, this painting is still in the artist's "Venetian" style as evidenced by the three-quarter-face figures and the joyful mood of the scene, bathed in dewy light and filled with subtle movement and delicately contrasting reflections and shadows. The group is aligned to form a sort of wedge, stretching away towards the back in a series of oblique lines. Diana's staff, the central and foremost point of the picture, relates explicitly with its slanting position to the two protagonists and the satyrs. In contrast, the handmaids close the right side of the composition, the three figures standing perfectly straight with tranquil faces. The radiant goddess, the portly, easy-going Silenus and their lively, attractive companions alternate with a mass of decorative detail: fruit shining like jewels, delicate little birds, furry game and excited hunting dogs. These "secondary" yet important elements in the structure of the picture are recognizable as the work of Frans Snyders. They blend perfectly with the festive sensuality of the painting which in itself is a real hymn to the joy of living. They are a necessary and integral part of the theme, and not just a decorative element. (L.C.R.)

PIETER PAUL RUBENS. *Mercury and Argos.*

This is a sketch for a panel in the royal apartments at Torre de la Parada, for the decoration of which in 1636 Rubens was assigned the Herculean task of painting twenty-five rooms with mythological scenes (mostly from Ovid's *Metamorphoses*). Helped by the faithful Frans Snyders, he worked on the commission for two years. Then, after his death, it was continued by Jordaens.

This "first idea," entirely by Rubens, is very different from both the final painting in Madrid and a related sketch in Brussels. In the latter two, Mercury stands in the foreground about to strike the sleeping Argos with his sword. Here, however, there is a quite different handling of the subject, depicting an earlier part of the story, when the god with his pipe lulls asleep the unbending guardian of the cow. (Io was transformed into a cow through the jealousy of Hera.)

The tree at the center in both versions has particular formal significance. Placed further back into the ample background of thickets and clearings in the final version, its trunk and knotty branches reflect the figure and gesture of Mercury. Here an integral part of the rocky foreground, it supports the heavy body of the sleeper, who leans against its trunk and roots, almost fusing with them. It seems to become an extension of him and take on his slumbering vitality in the shimmering movement of its leaves and branches.

It has quite rightly been observed that in this superb rendering of the pantheism of antiquity a single life force animates both god and tree, man and cow. The rounded shapes in the powerful body of the cow with its shining white skin, are admirably composed, and the tranquil stare of the beast, with muzzle thrust forward, at once watchful and patient, forms an emotional element of the story.

Behind the diagonal formed by the protagonists the sky appears as if on fire, with the golden reflections of the setting sun on the clouds and on the background landscape—the bare slopes of which slant down to the distant plain in a diagonal movement repeating that of the foreground figures themselves. The extraordinary

PIETER PAUL RUBENS
Siegen, Westphalia 1577—Antwerp 1640
Mercury and Argos (ca. 1635–38)
Oil on panel; 24¾″ x 34½″.
Inv. no. 962

unity of composition and pictorial significance is emphasized by the warmth and spread of color harmonies—a haze of gold, reddish streaks, and violet shadows superimposed on the basic rusty browns of the earth and the tree trunks: the luminous greens, the white Io, the flesh-pinks all overlaid with shadows and reflections, which are as it were summed up and symbolized in Mercury's short red cloak. (L.C.R.)

ANTHONY VAN DYCK. *Drunken Silenus*. *p. 84*
The heavy body of the intoxicated old man projects forward, forming a disjointed axis as the main element in the composition. His precariously unsteady pose, and the rather schematized diagonal and horizontal forms described by his strong arms and large, heavy torso contrast with the more regular vertical forms at either side: the beautiful supporting female figure on the left and the young man and the negro on the right. This very early work provides an instance (rarer than is generally claimed) of van Dyck's borrowing of motifs and forms from Rubens, although in depicting the court of Silenus he avoids an unctuous, viscous impasto in favor of a manner which sweetens and prettifies the mythological subject. It was a natural borrowing for the younger artist to make, humbly awed as he was by his famous

83

ANTHONY VAN DYCK
Antwerp 1599—London 1641
Drunken Silenus (before 1621)
Oil on canvas; 42″ x 36″.
Signed top center on the jug, "AVD"
Inv. no. 1017

ANTHONY VAN DYCK
Antwerp 1599—London 1641
The Children of Charles I (ca. 1636)
Oil on canvas; 51½″ x 59½″.
Inv. no. 1033

master's example. The sense of restrained savageness and van Dyck's characteristic soft silver light which imbues the whole create a sense of rarefied beauty—the intricate disorder of the soft foliage, the silver highlights of Silenus's curling hair, the sensuous figure and the glowing locks of his supporter, in the splendid abandon of her pose evoking the mystical languor of the Magdalene; and finally—in the recognizable style of the artist—the long, slender hands, their aristocratic elegance contrasting with the fat shoulders of the helpless old man. (L.C.R.)

ANTHONY VAN DYCK. *The Children of Charles I.*
This is a replica of the picture now in Windsor dated 1635. Official painter of the royal court and English aristocracy between 1632 and 1641, van Dyck has left us a

ANTHONY VAN DYCK
Antwerp 1599—London 1641
Portrait of a Man in Armor with a Red Armband
(1627–1631)
Oil on canvas; 35⅜" x 27⅞".
Inv. no. 1026

long series of portraits which reveal the empty pomp and irresponsible courage of
the contemporary society in the face of imminent collapse and its perverse refusal
to understand its own responsibilities.

The artist often had the help of collaborators to finish the numerous portraits
he was asked to paint at this time—as evident in this particular work.

There are a number of van Dyck portraits—most of them now in England—of
the elegant, fragile and innocent little figures, the children of Charles I. In this version, the three eldest (Charles, Mary and James) stand between two lateral uprights
which function as a symmetrical frame and direct the eye toward the center, in a
triangular positioning of the figures which is accented by two little dogs, one on either side of the group. The precious silk costumes worn by the children seem almost to assume an equal, if not greater importance than their firm little bodies and
round young faces. (L.C.R.)

ANTHONY VAN DYCK. *Portrait of a Man in Armor with a Red Armband.*
This portrait, executed spontaneously, probably without preliminary drawings, is
one of the rare occasions when the artist, working on impulse, deliberately attempt-
ed to create an impression of decisiveness and energetic will. Viewed in a rotating
movement but with hand solidly resting on a staff, the head turned in full-face in a
momentary pose, as indicated by the side glance of the eyes, this unknown warrior
has been endowed by the artist with a restless but controlled and youthful self-as-
surance which gives the picture a remarkable psychological intensity, outstanding
among the prodigious output of portraits by van Dyck.

The artist's particular gift as a colorist is much in evidence in the dramatic contrasts of the face and the red sash against the dark, uniform background; and above
all the play of light and reflections on the metal cuirass, sparkling over the em-
bossed and welded plate in a thousand different ways, creating a beautiful, delicate

and intricate pattern. This armor motif was a recurrent theme in van Dyck's work as can be seen in the early painting of *St. Martin* (Saventham and Windsor), and in the magnificent trappings of *Thomas of Savoy* (Turin) and of *Charles I* (Windsor, Petersburg etc.).

The Dresden portrait was probably painted in the artist's Antwerp period after his travels in Italy in 1727–31, when he created so many of his most powerful and nobly romantic works. (L.C.R.)

JACOB JORDAENS
Antwerp 1593—Antwerp 1678
Diogenes with His Lantern, in the Market Place
(1642)
Oil on canvas; 91¾" x 137⅞".
Inv. no. 1010

JACOB JORDAENS. *Diogenes with His Lantern, in the Market Place.*
Though bearing no signature or date, this is an autograph work of Jordaens, painted in 1742, as confirmed by the existence of a signed and dated preparatory drawing (now in the Leroy Collection).

A work of the artist's mature years, this painting presents a mass of tumultuous forces held together by a strong formal logic and great psychological depth in the attitudes and faces of the numerous characters—by turns vulgarity, stolidity, doubt, indifference, malice and conceit are all portrayed. Deeply expressive is the central column-like figure of the philosopher, standing as straight and firm as the heavy staff on which he leans, which give added emphasis to the vertical axis of the composition—symbolizing the certitude that moral awareness can bring in the face of the incomprehension and derision of the masses. Jordaens avoids ornamental and descriptive digressions and holds together the prolific mass of his material—

88 the prodigious crowd of bystanders, the patient animals, the abundant fruit and

JAN WILDENS
Antwerp 1586—Antwerp 1653
Winter Landscape with a Hunter
Oil on canvas; 76⅜" x 115".
Signed and dated bottom left: JAN WILDENS.
FECIT. 1624
Inv. no. 1133

vegetables—in a solid structural unity, full of a remarkably coherent means of expression and meaning. (L.C.R.)

JAN WILDENS. *Winter Landscape with a Hunter*.
Signed and dated 1624 when the artist was about forty years old, this is one of his few dated works to survive and is certainly his masterpiece.

Jan Wildens' work offers an intelligent and sensitive reflection of the great painting of Rubens though it lacks the master's magical unity of form, intense lyricism and at times almost savage frenzy of improvisation. Wildens, however, retains Rubens' breadth of form and ease of composition. These come together in that precise and ordered symmetry which is a constant feature of Wildens' work and which, indeed, becomes almost monotonous at times. This landscape, conceived and executed in great depth and seen as an end in itself, is developed on two distant planes: the first comprises the figure of the huntsman with his dogs and the balancing mass of shrubs and great thick tree trunks; the second is a snowy plain suffused with a smooth, even, yellowish light. (L.C.R.)

89

JAMES ENSOR. *Curly Cabbage.*

Painted in 1890, this work belongs to Ensor's most fertile and creative period, following the large *Entry of Christ* in Brussels by two years, and dating from the same year as *The Intrigue* and other famous pictures. Already as early as 1880 Ensor had been painting still lifes on tables covered with table-cloths—vases, fans, dead game, chinoiserie objects, shells and many other singular objects appeared on his canvases. Besides these there were also vegetables, as in this painting which is similar in its arrangement to other works both before and after it. Even if his style is best expressed in bizarre, far-off visions of crowds, skeletons or masks, in which the brushstroke is more spontaneous, the color more explosive, and the fantasy more elevated, even in his still lifes he is able to illustrate his dictum that "everything is worth painting since everything is beautiful and good to paint." The choice of this subject matter also reflects Ensor's desire to continually widen his terms of reference, constantly searching for novelty in order to avoid the dangers of uninspired repetition. His characteristic love of color and brilliant light remain unchanged, as does his ability to convey the texture and feel of objects through an accomplished mastery and freedom of handling. (P.C.S.)

JAMES ENSOR
Ostend 1860—Ostend 1949
Curly Cabbage
Oil on canvas; 31½″ x 39⅜″.
Dated above right, 1890
Inv. no. 2617

90

DUTCH PAINTING
16th-19th Centuries

JOOS DE MOMPER THE YOUNGER. *Mountain Landscape with Water Mill and Church.*

It has rightly been said that this artist, a contemporary of Rubens, has the panoramic breadth of a Patinir. He is interested primarily in creating a sense of depth and achieves this by subtle variations of color through the series of planes which stretch back into the pale blue distance. Browns are almost always confined to the foreground, though they too are often lit by unexpected rays of light. Around the contours of trees this light is condensed into those little dots of yellow—prefiguring pointillism—which are the real signature of Momper's work. The whole of this painting is typical of the artist; its true protagonists are the distant valleys, the sunny hills and the dark rocks dropping away in the foreground. A few descriptive, anecdotal elements are added: the small, unobtrusive figures of travelers, horsemen, gypsies and huntsmen, all spread out in silent little groups almost as if they did not wish to disturb the solemnity of their surroundings. It is a well established fact that Momper almost always called in other painters to provide this type of animation which he considered a necessary but subsidiary addition. They also painted the houses, the mill and the little bridge and in other works provided additions like caves and waterfalls (see for example picture No. 868 in the Dresden Gallery which is one of the few works actually bearing the artist's signature). It is however, the great sweep of landscape which really dominates the picture; and more than the little foreground figures, the real signs of life are the birds flying freely and securely in the sky. (L.C.R.)

REMBRANDT. *Samson Posing the Riddle to the Wedding Guests.*   *pp. 94-95*

Signed and dated 1638. We know that during this period Rembrandt studied and often copied a print of Leonardo's *Last Supper*, concentrating particularly on the structural massing and the compositional solution adopted by Leonardo to depict the complex group of figures. But the theme of a table surrounded by numerous participants was developed over a hundred years later by the Dutch artist into a very different compositional type. In this respect it is worth noting the richness of clothing and furnishings, and the exotic atmosphere suggested by the hair-styles and the setting; also the massing of the groups around the central figure of the bride, which build up toward the right hand side into a large, wave-like form. The commanding figure in the composition has been carefully shifted off center toward the right, and has become the position from which the chiaroscuro effects of the whole emanate, the bride and the ornate plate in front of her bathed in a pool of light which falls on the table from the left. Notable is the reversed position of the groom who turns to pose the riddle to his guests, and, above all, the monumental pyramid of the passive bride, covered with silks and jewels, isolated and accentuated by the rich carpet against which she is set. Throughout the sumptuous atmosphere, which becomes the painter's hallmark in the following years, concentrated faces, bizarre headdresses, heavy pitchers and folds of drapery emerge from the darkness. Rembrandt illustrates the story at its most vital moment and joins its various strands into a fully united whole which has been described, quite rightly, as Shakespearean. (L.C.R.)

REMBRANDT. *Self-portrait with Saskia.*   *p. 96*

A signed work, this has usually been considered a self-portrait with the artist's young wife in the first happy days of their marriage, and therefore datable to about 1634. Recently the painting has been interpreted as "The Prodigal Son in an Inn," though in all probability it represents the artist and his wife, and this could have been purposely correlated with the Biblical episode. In any case the picture shows two carefree figures, lightheartedly immersed in a world of silks and feathers, velvet

Pp. 94–95

REMBRANDT HARMENSZ VAN RIJN

Leiden 1606—Amsterdam 1699
Samson Posing the Riddle to the Wedding Guests
Oil on canvas; 49¾" x 69".
Signed and dated at bottom center: Rembrandt f.
1638
Inv. no. 1560

JOOS DE MOMPER THE YOUNGER
Antwerp 1564—Antwerp 1635
Mountain Landscape with Water Mill and
Church
Oil on panel; 20¾" x 28¼".
Inv. no. 869

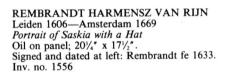

and fine carpets, the curtain on the right adding a suggestion of opulence, a still life of food and tableware on the left. The gay almost giddy atmosphere is unusual, and is emphasized by the equally rare lively coloring, and the strong, uniform lighting. This covers most of the scene except for the top and the bottom where deep shadows invade the scene which revolves around the oblique axis of the tall wineglass. (L.C.R.)

REMBRANDT. *Portrait of Saskia with a Hat.*
The earliest of the artist's many paintings in Dresden, this portrait shows the plump and smiling face of the twenty-one year old Saskia, shortly before her marriage. In this and the previous years Rembrandt painted quite a few portraits of his future wife, as well as a large number of other male and female portraits—mostly bust-length like this one—in oval or rectangular frames. This portrait illustrates some of the essential qualities of the master's early period—the rapid brush strokes, the use of light and shade which highlights only parts of the figure, leaving the rest in near darkness. Here the hat leaves the sitter's eyes and forehead in shade, while the light falls over her round face and her spontaneous yet somewhat malicious smile. The vertical elements—the ribbon bows on her shoulder, the delicately curved feather—and the horizontal ones consisting of the hat and its chain, and the lace veil drawn around her shoulders, combine to give an uneasy, momentary balance, which accentuates the fleeting, evocative quality of the whole. (L.C.R.)

97

REMBRANDT HARMENSZ VAN RIJN
Leiden 1606—Amsterdam 1669
Saskia Holding a Red Carnation
Oil on panel; 38¾" x 32½".
Signed and dated at bottom left: Rembrandt f.
1641.
Inv. no. 1562

REMBRANDT. *Saskia Holding a Red Carnation.*
A faded signature with the date 1641 indicates that this is probably the last portrait of Saskia van Uylenburch, the painter's rich, fragile wife. The loss of her children, her difficult life with a good but extravagant man, the disease from which she was presumably suffering and which led to her death in the following year, have not altered her slightly listless, plump beauty, which in the double portrait of six or seven years earlier was smiling light-heartedly. Rembrandt displays a fine mastery of tone, creating an evocative, dreamy atmosphere suggestive of hidden passion, deepening the warm, golden light on his wife's rich, loose clothing. One hand presses a shawl against her breast, the other offers a red flower; her smile is satisfied, if slightly uncertain, her shining eyes are a little absent, creating a sadly melancholic effect reminiscent of a figure on an Athenian grave stele. (L.C.R.)

REMBRANDT. *The Abduction of Ganymede.*
In the Dresden Cabinet of Drawings there is a remarkable preparatory sketch, a very good example of the spontaneity of Rembrandt's graphic imagination, especially as compared to more academic, standardized representation. It is worth noting how rarely it is that one of his many drawings can be related to a finished painting; usually they reflect ideas which later might be loosely adopted by him. In this example, instead, the drawing shows the group of the eagle and child exactly as transposed to canvas, wherein the artist depicts the subject with an intentionally

REMBRANDT HARMENSZ VAN RIJN
Leiden 1606—Amsterdam 1669
The Abduction of Ganymede
Oil on canvas; 67½" x 51".
Signed and dated on the drapery: Rembrandt. fe
1635
Inv. no. 1558

REMBRANDT HARMENSZ VAN RIJN
Leiden 1606—Amsterdam 1669
Self-Portrait with a Bittern
Oil on panel; 47½″ x 35″
Signed and dated 1638.
Inv. no. 1561

biting realism, parodying the mythological account. The powerful eagle rises up from the earth, bearing the pitiful infant to the merciless elements, his agonizing lot fully expressed in the grimacing expression on his crying face and the way his hand still clutches the cherries he was playing with seconds before being carried off. The group is isolated in the open air in the center of the canvas, arranged in a "T"-shape beneath the eagle's great symmetrical wings, in the full light of the sun. Beyond, a storm-ridden sky toward which Zeus flies, merges with a lifeless and colorless landscape, marked only by haunting, strangely shaped trees. (L.C.R.)

REMBRANDT. *Self-Portrait with a Bittern.*

Perhaps the most expressive of the artist's self-portraits, this is considered by many to be an experiment in the effects of light and shade, to which Rembrandt was devoting a great deal of attention during this period. Light streams in, highlighting certain particular points, and, through reflected light, defining the background with a warm, life-giving glow. The light which falls over the feathers of the bird—probably a bittern—and the sharp, almost metallic claws, is diffused in the plane behind, over the face, the folds of the collar, the large brown cloak and the deep background. Some shadowy objects are picked out by an occasional ray of light—a cheek, a wall, or the edge of a cloak. In short, it is a study which is a bold challenge and a masterly solution of the representation of bodies and objects in light, shadow and darkness, resolved with incredible audacity and modernity, all the more expressive because its main elements are traditional and can be found throughout Rembrandt's work. The same facial type is shared by many of the portraits which span his career from a boy of thirteen until old age, while the pose is a straight-forward frontal one; even the central feature, the dead bird, can be found in the two still lifes with young girls, in Amsterdam and in the Bührle collection in Zürich. (L.C.R.)

JOHANNES VERMEER. *Girl Reading a Letter.*   *p. 102*

Datable around 1657, this is the first of a long series of studies by the artist all based on the theme of a single figure illuminated by the light of a window. The girl's pure profile stands out against the flat, uniform background of the wall, with a sense of simplicity which occurs throughout Vermeer's work. The break between the interior, with the isolated, absent figure of the girl and her reflection in the window—recalling a van Eyckian "picture within a picture"—and the barrier in the foreground formed by the carpet and the still-life, has led many to define this as two separate subjects, joined only by the flowing curtain. It is, however, a picture singularly unified by the pervading light, which is reflected around the room, and as if glowing from within the objects themselves. The high vanishing point helps give the scene the character of a carefully contrived "tableau," while the clear, bright light heightens the sense of silence, isolation and peace. Luminous silks,

JAN (JOHANNES) VERMEER
Delft 1632—Delft 1675
Girl Reading a Letter (ca. 1657)
Oil on canvas; 32¼" x 25½".
Illegible signature at center right.
Inv. no. 1336

warm and richly embroidered velvets, soberly elegant furnishings and the quiet, absorbed figure combine to make an enclosed, coherent whole in which an everyday event acquires the solemn and imperishable grandeur of a classical statue. (L.C.R.)

JOHANNES VERMEER. *The Procuress.*
Of the various proposed identifications of the sitters the most probable is that it is the artist with his wife Catherine Bolnes (married 1653) and his shrewd mother-in-law Maria. As one of the masterpieces of Vermeer's developing years it has been much studied in order to clarify the formation of his style. The chiaroscuro effects and the pose of the musician derive from Rembrandt, possibly through Karel Fabritius; the lighting is distantly suggestive of the direct shadows of Caravaggio's candlelight, though it depends more on the juxtaposition of strong local colors in full light; above all, the subject, on a theme of sinful transgression related to the parable of the Prodigal Son, is typical among the artists of Utrecht.

The four half-figures around the table, in the luminous tones and instinctive purity which ennoble all the artist's creations, are arranged in four overlapping

102

JAN (JOHANNES) VERMEER
Delft 1632—Delft 1675
The Procuress
Oil on canvas; 56¼" x 50".
Signed and dated at bottom right: J V Meer
1656
Inv. no. 1335

FRANS HALS
Antwerp c. 1580—Haarlem 1666
Portrait of a Man
Oil on panel; 9¾″ x 7¾″.
Inv. no. 1358

planes, enclosed in a space defined by two triangular groups, a dark one on the left composed of the musician and his cape and a lighter one made up of the two lovers on the right. Vermeer, as always concerned with the ordering and composition of his canvas, further divides the whole into two horizontal parts—below, the oriental carpet, which echoes the colors of the rest of the composition; and above, the group of figures, seen slightly from below, their colorful clothes set off against the monochrome background, transforming this "trivial scene" into a joyful, serene feast of color. (L.C.R.)

FRANS HALS. *Portrait of a Man.*
This man, with his green jacket and spontaneous, ironically smiling glance, is typical of a long series of bust-length portraits by Hals, all set against neutral backgrounds and none containing much indication of the subject's occupation or class. This continuous series began in 1611 with the portrait of Jacob Zaffius and carried on into the artist's final years, when the style became livelier and more vibrantly dramatic. The sitter of this portrait, usually dated between 1630 and 1635, is identified in a print by W. Baille of 1765 as the artist himself. It is in fact quite close to

104

PHILIPS DE KONINCK
Amsterdam 1619—Amsterdam 1688
Landscape
Oil on canvas; 65″ x 48″.
Inv. no. 1612A

the known self-portrait in *The Banquet of the Officers of the St. George Militia Company*, although similar features are shared by many of Hals's sitters. If it is a self-portrait, Hals's age—he was born some time before 1585—would date it at least ten years earlier than generally accepted. This would in fact suit the style of the painting—the thick, rapid brush strokes, the use of black to moderate the sharper tones of the palette all suggesting a date between 1624 and 1627. Also typical of that period is the simplicity of the pose, made up of a few basic elements treated with a certain bravura and elegance—for instance the fine lace collar set off against the rich watered texture of the sitter's clothes. (L.C.R.)

PHILIPS DE KONINCK. *Landscape.*
Koninck, one of Rembrandt's pupils, is among the earliest masters of the so-called "inverted landscape," in which there are no features to hold one's attention while the sky becomes all important—for which the Dutch school is famous. By choosing a high viewpoint Koninck has kept the horizon line within the lower half of the canvas. The horizontal bands of land and water, crossed here and there by sand dunes or lines of trees, emphasize the breadth of the landscape, while the sky ap-

105

pears even more spacious, with lowering banks of clouds moving freely over the ordered expanse of the land which, vast and silent, bears all the marks of human cultivation. (L.C.R.)

JOB BERCKHEYDE. *The Interior of the Groote Kerk in Haarlem.*

The influence of Hans Vredeman de Vries and his theoretical writings on perspective and Baroque decoration is clearly visible among the earlier seventeenth-century Dutch architectural painters. Although these representations became quite conventional, painted with an almost geometric precision, scenes like this one by Job Berckheyde—of Haarlem's main church—derive their peculiar appeal from the contrast between the simplicity and clarity of the large-scale architectural elements and the crowd of tiny figures these enclose, bringing the normal life of the everyday world into the sacred confines of the church. A pupil of his more famous brother, Job stresses the contrasts of light and shade throughout the vast interior, leaving the arched ceiling in a near darkness corresponding to the long shadows across the floor of the nave. Shifting the perspective axis to the right, he reduces that side of the nave to five columns bathed in light, while on the other side views open up between the columns, in a subtle articulation of space and chiaroscuro. (L.C.R.)

PHILIPS WOUWERMAN. *Cavalry Skirmish in Front of a Burning Windmill.*

This picture, from the famous Crozat Collection, is signed at the bottom "Phils

JOB BERCKHEYDE
Haarlem 1630—Haarlem 1693
The Interior of the Groote Kerk in Haarlem
Oil on panel; 24" x 33½".
Signed and dated at bottom right: J. Berckheyde 1665
Inv. no. 1511

PHILIPS WOUWERMAN
Haarlem 1619—Haarlem 1668
*Cavalry Skirmish in Front of a Burning
Windmill*
Oil on canvas; 21½″ x 26″.
Inv. no. 1463

W.'' In the foreground are depicted horsemen and soldiers engaging in battle on a small patch of plain beneath a wide expanse of sky full of smoky white clouds. Thus within a typical "inverted landscape," two-thirds of which is sky—common in Holland, especially in the Haarlem school, after the innovations of Jan van Goyen—we have a lively, objective account of a contemporary event: a confused battle scene, the excited movements of horses and men interspersed with blackish smoke and fierce reflections of the blaze.

These two kinds of painting fail to blend into a unified image of struggle and destruction, but remain distinct, never transcending the impersonal, detached quality of craftsmanship, however professionally exercised, and convention, however cleverly employed and animated. It is a late work of the artist and illustrates the limitations of his inspiration, which only occasionally, in some simpler, more modest pictures, seems to take flight—away from simple rhetorical technique such as this, which despite its movement and wealth of detail remains essentially somewhat ostentatious. (L.C.R.)

107

JACOB VAN RUISDAEL
Haarlem 1628/9—Haarlem 1678
The Jewish Cemetery near Ouderkerk
Oil on canvas; 33″ x 37½″.
Signed at bottom left: J v Ruisdael
Inv. no. 1502

JACOB VAN RUISDAEL. *The Jewish Cemetery near Ouderkerk.*
The conflict between an intensely emotional vision and a wish to avoid romantic interpretation explains Ruisdael's predilection for tormented views, blasted oak trees, deserted ruins and landscapes where the powerful forces of nature have been unchained. Filled with evocative and poetic motifs is his *Cemetery*, a dark, agitated vision pervaded with melancholy, centered on the bright white marble tombstone which stands out in sharp contrast against the gloomy, uncertain gray-green-brown tones of the ruins, clouds and trees which surround it. The contorted branches of the dead tree at the right, frozen in the shape of a lightning bolt, rise to the menacing sky like some sort of cry of pain, an accusing, despairing plea. This highly suggestive vision has inspired varying responses and iconographic interpretations from many, including Goethe. To our generation, after the Nazi atrocities, this desolate vision of death and forsaken life might well seem like a presage of the suffering and persecution of Dutch Jews in this century. (L.C.R.)

109

GERARD TERBORCH. *Lady Washing her Hands.*
It has been justifiably noted that in Terborch's portrayals of the elegant society of his day—while never falling into the amorphous banality of "photographic truth"—everyday actions are treated with a simple immediacy which precludes any complex psychological overtones. The lady in profile at the center is placed against a minutely described background built up of rectangles—the paintings, the carpet and the four poster bed. All is clearly and sharply delineated, in complete contrast with the far more suggestive *Portrait of a Young Man*, also in Dresden, in which the subject is seen from behind, emerging from the mysterious shadows of his room. Even here, though, the characters reveal nothing of their thoughts or feelings, totally absorbed as they are in their daily occupations. (L.C.R.)

WILLEM CLAESZ HEDA. *Breakfast Table with Blackberry Pie.*
Although all these objects are minutely described in glistening detail the whole achieves a coherent unity which is not broken down by the parts. Within the limpid clarity of the atmosphere, placed in an arrangement of complex diagonals, the ob-

GERARD TERBORCH
Zwolle 1617—Deventer 1681
Lady Washing her Hands (ca. 1665)
Oil on panel; 21″ x 17″.
Signed on back of book at left: G T Borch
Inv. no. 1830

WILLEM CLAESZ HEDA
Haarlem 1594—Haarlem 1680/82
Breakfast Table with Blackberry Pie
Oil on panel; 21¼″ x 32¼″.
Signed and dated at bottom center: Heda. 1631.
Inv. no. 1371

jects become part of a whole made one by the lighting. The broken glass, the rough-ly sliced pie and its half-eaten remains, the tablecloth folded back, the open pocket watch and the fallen cup all suggest the sudden interruption of a meal. But they are all no more than pretexts for chromatic contrasts and effects of light, a unified pic-torial whole which, while based on *trompe-l'oeil* techniques, becomes more impor-tant than its parts in an ambience of exalted luminosity which matches Vermeer's. (L.C.R.)

ADRIAEN VAN OSTADE
Haarlem 1610—Haarlem 1685
Self-Portrait of the Artist in his Studio
Oil on panel; 15″ x 14″.
Signed and dated at bottom right: Av. Ostade.
1663
Inv. no. 1397

ADRIAEN VAN OSTADE. *Self-Portrait of the Artist in his Studio.*
Dated 1663, this is a late work of the artist, who along with Brouwer, was a pupil
of Hals. Strongly influenced by Rembrandt, through his own great skills Brouwer
was a key figure in the development of seventeenth-century Dutch genre painting in
its representation of everyday life. In this painting of the artist at work, which is be-
lieved to be a self-portrait, he expresses his varied artistic aspirations. The scene becomes a statement of the artist's status, his circumstances and the vicissitudes
which afflict him. The light filters through the brilliantly rendered window into the
room which is composed of successive planes, like the insertions of "pictures within
a picture." These secondary pictures include not only the landscape being painted—significantly enough on an easel in a studio—and other canvases and drawings
lying around, but also the bent figure of the color-grinder on the raised floor at the
far end of the room reduced in the gloomy distance to no more than a shadow, an
effect reminiscent of Brouwer's works of a few years earlier. Scattered about are
disparate objects which will become the basis of finely calculated effects of coloring
and composition—jugs, drapery, statues, and so forth—in addition to the artist's
tools, brushes, canvases and panels, frames, and a dummy figure. Above the window hangs a dusty curtain to modify the light, which flows into the room bathing it
with the soft, warm glow of a summer evening. (L.C.R.)

GERARD DOU. *Self-Portrait of the Artist in his Studio.*   *p. 114*
Dou, in total contrast to van Ostade, shows himself surrounded by a mass of objects: sculptures, draperies, vases, as well as musical instruments, a globe, a lamp.
They are all beautiful, clean, and shining—a self-satisfying collection of ostentatious opulence which by its very excess makes one somewhat suspicious. Dou,
when barely fifteen, became the first of Rembrandt's many pupils, developing as
one of his minor followers though at the same time popularizing his style for a wid-
er public. The dispersion of interest over such a multitude of objects mechanically
depicted, his taste for the literal, his magnifying-glass realism all too often detract
from his otherwise pleasing works any feeling of spontaneity or emotion. This picture of a young man preoccupied with his outward appearance and conscious of his
worldly success is psychologically revealing. (L.C.R.)

ADRIAEN BROUWER
Oudernaarde 1605/6—Antwerp 1638
Peasants Brawling
Oil on panel; 10½″ x 13½″.
Inv. no. 1059

GERARD DOU
Leiden 1613—Leiden 1675
Self-Portrait of the Artist in his Studio
Oil on panel; 17″ x 13¾″.
Signed and dated near the table at left: G DOV
1647
Inv. no. 1704

ADRIAEN BROUWER. *Peasants Brawling.*

A pupil of Hals, Brouwer produced a large and constant flow of works throughout his short, somewhat eccentric career. Characteristic of his art is his pure sense of color, immersed in a dark and mysterious background, his terse, straightforward scenes of a life without pretense, his abrupt honesty in his depictions of a miserable and suffering humanity, and his strong mastery of composition. All these are fully expressed in this scene of *Peasants Brawling.* The bare, dirty wall of the hovel serves as the smoky setting for the turquoises, greens and browns of the peasants' clothes, the white of the rag and the gray-green of the jug. In the dark corner near the fire two old people turn their wrinkled faces, their bent, broken bodies hunched up in contrast to the senseless, destructive energy of the brawlers. The latter are placed off-center, their wild movements confined within a tightly knit triangular mass which extends both vertically and in depth. Their arrangement in different planes, their distorted bodies and grimacing expressions demonstrate how "ignoble" subject matter—as it was termed in its day—could be expressed in a severely formal, luminous idiom. (L.C.R.)

115

VINCENT VAN GOGH
Groot Zundert 1853—Auvers-sur-Oise 1890
Still Life of Pears (1888)
Oil on canvas; 18″ x 23⅜″.
Inv. no. 2593

VINCENT VAN GOGH. *Still Life of Pears.*

In February 1888 van Gogh left Paris for Arles, where some of his most famous masterpieces were painted and where, at the end of that year, he had his row with Gauguin. This *Still Life*, painted during that autumn, is unique in its subject matter, comparable only to some sketches painted a few months earlier and later, early in 1889. Stylistically, however, the painting shows all the characteristics of his late years, when, as if with foreboding of the coming tragedy, van Gogh seemed almost possessed with an uncontrollable anxiety and creative tension, and, never satisfied with the results, lived in and for painting as if this constituted his only means of understanding and coming to terms with the world around him. Even these pears—which seem almost to melt into one another—have become an important part of his surroundings, together with the other objects that made up his world: people, the furniture in his room, the fields outside, the rivers, and the trees blossoming in spring. His nervous, erratic brush uneasily fixes and condenses the image, although he does not reach the same intensity of disturbed vision as in his more extreme paintings of Saint-Rémy and Auvers. (P.C.S.)

FRENCH PAINTING
17th-19th Centuries

NICOLAS POUSSIN. *The Kingdom of Flora.*

This picture was painted in 1631 for the adventurer Fabrizio Valguarnera, who was a great admirer of Poussin. It accordingly dates from one of the artist's most productive periods and one in which his study of contemporary and historical experience was at its most intense, namely the years he spent as a young man in Rome.

The picture is a hymn both to the heroes of Ovid's *Metamorphoses* and to the dazzling beauty of nature—the delicate loveliness and fragility of flowers. It has been compared, rather astutely, to a line of Alexandrine verse, the graceful, dancing figure of Flora as central caesura, with the separate yet harmoniously balanced figures around her ranged like the rest of the line. Advancing diagonally down from the left appear one by one the rigid form of Hermes, the tottering figure of Ajax and the beautiful circle formed by the bending bodies of Narcissus and the enamored Echo standing out in relief against the steep face of the rock. Then on the right in two planes are the group of Smilax and the nymph Crocus, united in a sinuous embrace, and behind two ephebic youths, in all probability Hyacinth and Adonis. Above, on a dense bank of clouds in the top center is the chariot of the Sun, enveloped in a magic circle of shining light. A narrow trellis leads down from the right, above the low blue line of hills, then turns at right angles to run along the back of the picture and form a sort of cornice around the dancing figures. Within it the dance continues, alive with contrasting rhythms and movements.

The subtle web of glittering highlights, the rich mythological content and the vaguely "Manneristic" flavor of the whole painting have led many scholars to compare it with the work of Primaticcio and in general with the style of decoration at Fontainebleau which is known to have impressed Poussin greatly in his youth. (L.C.R.)

NICOLAS POUSSIN. *Pan and Syrinx.*

Though several times repeated (Poussin was copied and imitated from the beginning of his career and increasingly as his fame grew, especially after his death), the

NICOLAS POUSSIN
Les Andelys 1594—Rome 1665
The Kingdom of Flora (1631)
Oil on canvas; 52″ x 71⅞″.
Inv. no. 719

NICOLAS POUSSIN
Les Andelys 1594—Rome 1665
Pan and Syrinx (ca. 1637)
Oil on canvas; 42″ x 32″.
Inv. no. 718

119

Dresden painting is universally accepted as the original, the one which Poussin himself tells us in a letter to Stella was executed around 1637 for a French painter, La Fleur.

The Ovidian theme conforms closely to other favorite and much painted subjects of Poussin's—*Apollo and Daphne*, the *Shepherds in Arcadia, Bacchus and the Nymphs*. It lends itself particularly to one of those miraculous assemblages of bodies and tree trunks, flowers and shrubs, in which both the significance of the story and the visual narration of it, however minute the details, are subordinated to a profound, controlled intellectual *pathos* deriving solely from the disposition of the motifs, the gestures, the cadenced attitudes of the bodies: not unlike Greek sculpture and vase painting, as has been observed.

Poussin's erudite visual orchestration resolves the key moment, with Syrinx being simultaneously pursued and rescued, in a movement of suspended dance, slanting down toward the curious nymph on the left. The two putti in the foreground, also caught at a precarious equilibrium, provide an opposite diagonal toward the right. The lively, briskly moving figures are captured within the tightly enclosed circular area defined by the slender tree trunks, which are disposed like an open portico against the immobile, luminous landscape of sky, clouds, mountains and greenery in the background.

Another version of the same subject, with the protagonists among the trees and reeds on the bank of the river Ladon, now survives only in an engraving by Bernard Picard dated 1724. The Dresden Gallery also has a Poussinesque *Sacrifice to Pan*, the work of an Italian artist, similar to Castiglione. (L.C.R.)

NICOLAS POUSSIN. *Adoration of the Magi.*

Signed and dated Rome 1633, this is a celebrated painting (there exist numerous copies of it, in the Louvre, Dulwich College Picture Gallery, etc.) which can justly be regarded as a major work of Poussin from the third decade of the seventeenth century.

The design is quite complex. The adoring figures represented as heroes from the classical world without any reference to the East, are masterfully grouped in a fluid tangle of bodies and brightly colored clothes in the foreground, in sharp contrast with the clear geometrical structure in the left background. At the upper right appears the most natural action of the picture, where the angel's announcement has caused what looks like a homely scene outside a cottage in the Roman countryside.

The whole is an excellent example of a real search for perfection, not just through careful drawing but through meticulous attention to the slow and thoughtful process of realizing his design, which is the peculiar characteristic of Poussin's art. His hand is at times impatient to the extent of taking the most extraordinary risks but always remains firmly controlled by his "*raison*," and kept rigorously subject to the demands of his overall design. This plan is always calmly considered and carefully constructed; his execution pays continual attention to every facet of past and present experience. All this constitutes that "*capital de l'art*" to which Poussin always remained so staunchly faithful. (L.C.R.)

CLAUDE LORRAIN. *Landscape with the Flight into Egypt.* *p. 122*

The corresponding picture in the *Liber Veritatis* (no. 110) is signed and dated 1647. The name of the buyer is indicated as "*pour mr parasson a Lions.*" Parasson was probably an agent for Cardinal Mazarin who owned the picture from 1653 onwards. There are numerous versions of it, on the market, in private collections, and in the museums of Melbourne and Stuttgart. In all probability it was painted at the same time as the *Pastoral Landscape* which is now in the Metropolitan Museum in New York. This would certainly be in keeping with the artist's well-known habit of creating his pictures in pairs, each one of the pair having the same measurements

NICOLAS POUSSIN
Les Andelys 1594—Rome 1665
Adoration of the Magi
Oil on canvas; 63⅜″ x 71¾″.
Signed and dated bottom right, on the drum of
the column: Accad: rom. NICOLAUS PUSIN
faciebat Romae. 1633.
Inv. no. 717

and horizon though otherwise being different in composition and lighting.

The landscape in this picture gives a great feeling of space, stretching back in horizontal lines of water and land to fade finally into the bluish distance of the mountains which can just be seen in the limpid morning light. This extraordinary quality of the air which is so characteristic of the work of Lorrain is here achieved with particular mastery through the exquisite alternation of the shadows and the reflections, and the delicate application of silvery tones which give further emphasis to the gradation of light.

As usual in the work of Lorrain the subject of the picture is secondary, serving almost entirely as a pretext for the great panoramic landscape. This is given some relevance, however, by the movements of the tiny yet exquisite figures, the refreshment offered by the sparkling water and the protective shade of the great trees. In a sense the whole of the landscape, with its serene and reassuring immensity, is a ma-

121

jestic evocation of the liberty and peace sought by the Holy Family in their flight toward a safer haven. (L.C.R.)

CLAUDE LORRAIN. *Landscape with Acis and Galatea.*   *p. 123*
This picture, which is signed and dated 1657, corresponds to No. 141 in the *Liber Veritatis*, where it is marked as painted *"pour Mr Delaga"* in Rome. There is a large drawing of the scene in the Royal Collection at Windsor. The painting was one of a pair; the other, *Metamorphosis of the Apulian Shepherd*, is now in the Ellesmere Collection. The figures were repainted by one of the Boulogne brothers, either Bon or Louis. The insertion of two lovers alone beneath the hanging curtain of a tent in the center of the picture seems to have been added simply as a somewhat superfluous mythological pretext (from Ovid's *Metamorphoses*) for the magnificent coastal landscape. In the top right quarter of the picture is the barely visible yet menacing presence of Polyphemus, posted on a rise in front of a smoking volcano in the far distance. More important and more significant are the two trees balancing the composition on the left, intertwined as if in imitation of the embrace of the lovers.

The vast sweep of the landscape fades gently into the towering mountains on the coast and the tranquil immensity of a sea disturbed only by two tiny boats as it breaks lazily against the gravelly shore. The whole picture is suffused with the calm golden light of the sun (not actually visible itself) which shines gently from the west; everything gives an impression of order, measured restraint, beauty, certainty and serenity. It is a dream landscape for the happy, mythical pair, but one which could become a reality if only men would not disturb the solemn magnificence of nature. (L.C.R.)

CLAUDE LORRAIN (CLAUDE GELLÉE)
Chamagne 1600—Rome 1682
Landscape with the Flight into Egypt
Oil on canvas; 40½" x 53⅛".
Signed and dated bottom left: CLAUDE IVEF
ROMA 1647
Inv. no. 730

CLAUDE LORRAIN (CLAUDE GELLÉE)
Chamagne 1600—Rome 1682
Landscape with Acis and Galatea
Oil on canvas; 40⅜" x 53½".
Signed and dated bottom right, next to a stone:
CLAUDE GELEE IVEF ROMA 1657
Inv. no. 731

ANTOINE WATTEAU. *Conversation in a Park.*   *pp. 124–125*

This picture was painted between 1715 and 1718, during the happiest and most productive years of the artist's life, when his friendship with Crozat had brought him into contact with new modes of expression and had given further force to his anti-academic inclinations. These inclinations had indeed been present in all his work even before this time; like his admiration for and real understanding of the work of Rubens, and the reflections in his work of the "Mannerism" of Fontaine-bleau, they were a result of his early association with the engraver Gérard Audran, that master of brilliantly inventive decoration and subtle, elegant arabesques.

Watteau very often chooses to depict a considerable number of characters, setting them in luxuriant natural surroundings, bathed in evanescent light which adds to the atmosphere of luxury, pleasure and lively enjoyment. This certainly contrasts with the sense of rigid etiquette and cool aloofness so often described by the chroniclers and historians of the time of Louis XIV. Watteau's is a world of conventions and illusions, created by means of imaginative rhythmic composition and theatrical stage settings, very much in the "grand manner." A number of elements in this *Conversation* underline the fact that the action is related to the theatre: the whole painting is rich in studied allusions to love expressed in the symbolic language of flowers; the step in the foreground seems almost formally to mark the proscenium; the figures of the "main characters" seem to have been carefully posed around the long marble bench in the full light, while a series of deepening golden reflections and subtle shadows gradually fade into the greenery of an unreal, ideal park in the background. There is one unusual touch, a sign of an almost ironic reaction on the part of the artist: a gentleman, tired of the endless chatter, prefers to stand apart and admire the magnificent figure of the Naiad. (L.C.R.)

ANTOINE WATTEAU
Valenciennes 1684—Nogent 1721
Conversation in a Park (ca. 1715–18)
Oil on canvas; 23⅞" x 29½".
Inv. no. 781

124

JEAN ETIENNE LIOTARD
Geneva 1702—Geneva 1789
The Chocolate Girl (Vienna, ca. 1743–45)
Pastel on parchment; 32½″ x 20⅝″.
Inv. no. P161

JEAN ETIENNE LIOTARD. *The Chocolate Girl.*

This seems to be the general public's favorite picture in the whole museum. The simple young woman stands enveloped in rigid modest clothes which, though given some attractiveness by the network of rippling folds, seem little more than a case from which emerge her rosy, shining, porcelain-like face and arms. The magnificent still life on the tray held in her delicate hands is enlivened by transparent reflections in the glass and water.

The faultless execution of this oversize "miniature" is a true masterpiece of illusionist art, a remarkable feat of *trompe-l'oeil*, on an exceptionally ample scale. The contrast between its size and the manner of its execution which retains the bright

MAURICE QUENTIN DE LA TOUR
St. Quentin 1704—St. Quentin 1788
Count Maurice of Saxony, Marshal of France
Pastel on paper; 23½" x 19¼".
Inv. P164

clear surface of the seventeenth-century miniatures together with all the magic of their delicate colors—particularly the predilection for white on white—gives a special interest to this beautiful picture which produces the effect of being seen through a magnifying glass, without movement, spirit or life. (L.C.R.)

MAURICE QUENTIN DE LA TOUR. *Count Maurice of Saxony, Marshal of France.*

One of the most perfect of the precious series of delicately rendered and subtly expressive pastels in which de la Tour depicted the Parisian society of the time of Louis XV, this early work offers an unusually intimate, "private" view of the famous, victorious commander. In the hint of a twinkle of his wise, sharp eyes, the absorbed but strangely vivacious face, and the sober yet richly refined and elegant clothes, the portrait is not simply that of a warrior but of a student of the art of warfare, the intelligent author of *Memoirs* and *Military Meditations*.

De la Tour made another portrait of the Marshal, this one in uniform, dating from a later period and now in the Louvre, where he is depicted with open expression and head held high, clothed sumptuously in damask and shining metal. In the Dresden Gallery there is also one by Liotard, in which this witty, experienced, well-read and highly cultured man is represented with nothing more than a conventionally unexpressive exterior, a mere symbol of power. (L.C.R.)

EDOUARD MANET
Paris 1832—Paris 1883
Portrait of Jeanne Martin, or *"The Woman in Pink"* (1881)
Oil on canvas; 35¾" x 28¼".
Signed at bottom left: Manet
Inv. no. 2598

EDOUARD MANET. *Portrait of Jeanne Martin (The Woman in Pink).*
Jeanne Martin, a friend of Forain's, worked for some time as a model in Manet's studio, where the artist painted a number of portraits of her. The three certain ones, of which the Dresden picture is one, were painted in 1881, and belong to a period when Manet, who died in 1883, executed a great many female portraits, of which the masterpiece is *The Bar of the Folies-Bergères.* The composition of this portrait recalls that of Méry Laurent, who symbolized Autumn in the unfinished series of the "Four Seasons."

The sitter here is a large, somewhat massive figure who completely dominates her surroundings, which are left bare of any other feature—if one excludes the chair-back which is in fact an essential part of the composition. The young woman's vitality is brought out in her attentively upheld head, which Manet has modeled with dry, rapid, direct and nervous brush strokes—note in particular the eyes, the ears, and the hair hanging over the forehead. In the same way, recalling the spontaneity of Velazquez' style, Manet draws the light folds of the dress, the bangles and the chair, never relaxing the liveliness and immediacy of his vision and execution. The pinks, blacks and browns constitute the most constant and characteristic chromatic effects of Manet's painting. (P.C.S.)

EDGAR DEGAS. *Two Ballet Dancers in Conversation.*   *p. 130*
From 1873 on Degas devoted a great deal of his work to the ballet, constantly visiting dancing schools and the Opéra, so much that the development of his style might be studied from this subject matter alone. These *Dancers*, of which there are four known variations, belong to the artist's last years, when, gradually losing his sight, he seems to have been obsessed with the idea of studying the movement of dance in all its possible attitudes and variations. A model was no longer necessary to him, considering that all the motions of ballet were by now deeply rooted in his imagination. Here, as in many other examples, the field of vision has been narrowed down so that the figures themselves make up the larger part of the composition which is articulated by the sharp angles and the contrapposto movements of their poses. Degas' old love for the Italian masters has not been forgotten; but here, displaying a new creative imagination, he adopts a field of powerful colors which mingle and spread, subsuming the angularity of the poses beneath the radiating

EDGAR DEGAS
Paris 1834—Paris 1917
Two Ballet Dancers in Conversation (ca. 1898)
Pastel on paper; 37⅞" x 34¼".
Signed bottom right: Degas
Inv. no. 2586

tones of reflected light. The finely balanced tension within the picture keeps Degas from falling into the danger of becoming repetitive or mannered. (P.C.S.)

CLAUDE MONET. *The Banks of the Seine at Lavacourt.*
In 1878, in order to escape his creditors, Monet left Argenteuil and settled in Vétheuil where he remained until November 1881. On the opposite bank of the Seine was the old village of Lavacourt where he often went to paint. Many of his landscapes during this period were executed on the banks of the river, which often enters into his compositions beside a road which curves into the distance, the houses of little hamlets, lines of trees and hills which close off the horizon. The Dresden painting is very close to another painted a year before in which one can see the same view, although the trees on the left are brought closer. The compositional scheme, related to Sisley's style, is based on a simple structural balance of horizontal and vertical elements which open up a large, open space at the center. The sense of communication and identification with nature, one of Monet's most important contributions to the Impressionist movement, is very strongly and warmly felt. His rapid, subtle brush strokes create a dynamic, moving atmosphere vibrating with color and light. Into this whole he is able to incorporate any figures or other narrative details which are incidental to the scene. (P.C.S.)

CLAUDE MONET
Paris 1840—Giverny 1929
The Banks of the Seine at Lavacourt (1879)
Oil on canvas; 26″ x 31½″.
Signed at bottom left: Claude Monet
Inv. no. 2525A

PIERRE AUGUSTE RENOIR. *Capitaine d'Arras.* *p. 132*
This portrait, painted when he was thirty, belongs to Renoir's early period. He had by then already met the people who were to remain his closest friends—Monet, Sisley and Bazille. He had also studied and assimilated the styles of Ingres, Courbet, Delacroix and Manet. It was in fact around 1870 that he himself was developing a fully individual style, as can be seen in this vigorous and intense portrait of the Capitaine d'Arras, whom Renoir met in Paris in the autumn of 1871. The whole figure lies in the plane of the canvas, in a vision characteristic of the artist, reflecting his expansive vitality. More than psychological insight, the portrait displays a rich

131

PAUL GAUGUIN
Paris 1848—Dominica, Marquesas Islands 1903
Two Seated Tahitian Women (Parau Api)
Oil on canvas; 26⅜" x 35¼".
Signed and dated at bottom right: Parau Api
[What News?] P Gaugin 92
Inv. no. 2610

PIERRE AUGUSTE RENOIR
Limoges 1841—Cagnes sur Mer 1919
Capitaine d'Arras
Oil on canvas; 31⅞" x 25⅝".
Signed and dated at bottom left: Renoir 71
Inv. no. 2608

use of color and brush stroke, particularly the ornately decorated jacket of the officer. The flaming color with effects of reflected light may hark back to the impetuous romanticism of Delacroix—whom Renoir was studying during this period—as can be seen in his other contemporary works such as the *Lady of Algiers* exhibited in the Salon of 1870. (P.C.S.)

PAUL GAUGUIN. *Two Seated Tahitian Women (Parau Api)*.
Executed during his first Tahitian visit, this is basically similar to the work under the same title in the Jeu de Paume in Paris. Far away from being savage or wild, as if he wanted to keep himself in Strindberg's tracks for as long as possible, Gauguin expresses himself with the fullness of his maturest period. His natural decorative sense, strengthened by the influence of the pure forms of Polynesian art, finds expression in the immediacy with which he arranges his composition, free from any naturalistic illusionism. None of the parts around the two main figures recede in depth, the whole reduced to a series of vividly colored, juxtaposed shapes, similar to the wide range of colored forms with which he experimented in Brittany. The self-conscious sense of primitivism derives from the broad, simplified handling of forms as well as his use of small detail. The painting becomes a statement, a refusal of the cheap values of civilization for a fully realized vision. (P.C.S.)

HENRI DE TOULOUSE-LAUTREC
Albi 1864—Malrome, Gironde 1901
The Two Friends
Oil on paper; 23½″ x 32″.
Signed and dated at bottom left:
HTL-autrec 1895
Inv. no. 2603

HENRI DE TOULOUSE-LAUTREC. *The Two Friends.*

Toulouse-Lautrec's fascination with lesbianism among prostitutes is reflected in the many drawings and paintings he made from his visits to the Parisian *maisons closes* from 1892 onwards. It is likely that the Dresden picture, like others of the same period, is based on sketches made on the spot in the Rue des Moulins. The two companions, shown at other times in moments of affection or conversation, are here seen resting. The scene is in fact dominated by the woman, unflatteringly observed and recorded, who sits at the center turning toward the artist. The space of the rest of the room is defined by two objects—the nude back of the second figure and the chair with the dress hanging over it. Although Lautrec's style developed in a largely idiosyncratic way one cannot but notice Degas' influence, which can be seen in the slightly distorted effects which stem from the angles at which the objects—in themselves making up a relatively simple composition—relate to one another. The skill and mastery of the whole is enough to dismiss those who pass off Lautrec as a facile artist, and shows instead how he could faithfully record the character and predicament of the world he portrayed, along with the exterior everyday appearance of his subjects. (P.C.S.)

SPANISH PAINTING
16th-17th Centuries

EL GRECO. *Christ Healing the Man Born Blind.*

This is a slightly later variation of a signed canvas which hangs in the art gallery in Parma, and was painted in Venice ca. 1572–1575. There is another, later version of the Parma canvas in New York's Wrightsman collection. This can be dated from the time of El Greco's stay in Spain where there are again two copies of it (Herran and Valle collections, Madrid).

El Greco had a well-known habit of repeating the same picture several times with a number of different variations, sometimes going back after decades to those *"originales"* which we know he kept in his studio and which recorded *"todo quanto había pintado en su vida"* (everything that he had painted in his life). It is evident that many of these themes served as models for pupils and collaborators, in many cases even after the death of the artist, so that distinguishing these from the works of the master is not always easy.

The Dresden version, however, is so substantially different in composition from any other that it seems unlikely that it is an impersonal, anonymous copy. The differences are not limited to simplifying the block of buildings in perspective on the left, clear geometrical outlines replacing the richly shaded colonnade, or bringing forward the two embracing figures thereby half obscuring the stair behind the protagonists. The very balance of the composition was altered: while in the Parma version Christ is in the center, in front of two very closely placed groups of bystanders, here two very similar groups are placed so as to form in plan, in conjunction with the two figures set back in the center, the three points of a rhombus which enclose the smooth stone floor of an empty central space. Christ stands nearest to the observer, at the fourth point of this rhombus. (L.C.R.)

EL GRECO (DOMENICOS
THEOTOKOPOULOS)
Fodele, Candia 1541—Toledo 1614
Christ Healing the Man Born Blind (Venice, ca.
1572–75)
Oil on panel; 26″ x 33″.
Inv. no. 276

DIEGO VELASQUEZ. *Portrait of Don Juan Mateos.* p. 138

This picture of Juan Mateos, Philip IV's Master of the Hunt, was painted around 1631-2, just after the young artist had returned from Italy, his head full of impressions and ideas gained from the works of the great Italian masters of the sixteenth century, particularly those of Titian.

The portrait exemplifies the superlative quality of perfect control, and the sudden flashes of brilliant improvisation, which provide unquestionable evidence of inspiration in Velasquez's work. The well-shaped imposing head, poised like a fragment of some classical marble on the stiff triangular base of the collar, stands out sharply in the diffused golden light which gives unity to the fluid, somber tones typical of the time. Velasquez makes no attempt to soften the strong harsh features of the Master of the Hunt, whose face accentuated by incisive modeling in light and shade, expresses an imposing, authoritative power. It has been said that a "Shakespearean" force of character typified the absolute and despotic monarchy of Philip IV, the class of people who surrounded him, and the whole tenor of the age. Certainly the artist has here centered attention on this type of power in the impervious lineaments of the unforgettable face of Juan Mateos. While simplification and spontaneous immediacy are characteristic of all Velasquez's work, here this simplification is particularly evident in the conventionality of the pose, in the sober, unvaried tone of the clothes and most particularly in the hands which, though their outlines are clearly defined, are themselves scarcely more than roughly sketched. (L.C.R.)

DIEGO RODRIGO DE SILVA Y VELAS-
QUEZ
Seville 1599—Madrid 1660
Portrait of Don Juan Mateos (ca. 1632)
Oil on canvas; 42¾" x 34¾".
Inv. no. 697

FRANCISCO DE ZURBARAN
Fuentes de Cantos 1598—Madrid 1664
St. Bonaventure Kneeling Before the Papal Crown
(1629)
Oil on panel; 93¾" x 87⅛".
Inv. no. 696

FRANCISCO DE ZURBARAN. *St. Bonaventure Kneeling before the Papal Crown.*

This picture was painted in 1628 for the College of St. Bonaventura in Seville, together with the *Visit of St. Thomas* (now destroyed, formerly in Berlin), *The Funeral Obsequies of the Saint* and *St. Bonaventure at the Council of Lyons* (the latter two now in the Louvre). Another four pictures were painted at the same time by Herrara the Elder.

The painting is an excellent example of those lyrical meditations on a monastic character which are so frequent in the work of Zurbaran. They are all variations on a constant of inspiration and formal plan, in which the melancholy reserve, the clear, powerful drawing, the exquisite colors contrasting sharply with dark backgrounds, the simplicity of the space and the logic of a composition severely based on rigorous geometric principles, all succeed in avoiding the monotony of any repetition or imitation.

In this youthful work the "realism" which is often cited as one of the painter's qualities, is, as always, subject to the geometric rigor of the composition: the closed cubic space, illuminated by the splendid light of the vision which strikes the face of the saint and continues over the clear sharp surfaces of his robe, the square planes of the tablecloth, the straight horizontal lines along which are ranged the figures of cardinals in the background outside, taking part in the election of the new pope; and in contrast, the dark mass of the cell wall. (L.C.R.)

JOSÉ DE RIBERA (LO SPAGNOLETTO)
Játiva di Valencia 1591—Naples 1652
St. Agnes in Prison
Oil on canvas: 80″ x 59⅞″.
Signed and dated below center: Jusepe de Ribera
español, F. 1641
Inv. no. 683

JOSÉ DE RIBERA. *St. Agnes in Prison.*

Painted in 1641, during the last years of Ribera's long stay in Naples, this picture of a lovely young girl solicitously protected by a kindly cherub is said to contain a likeness of the artist's young daughter. Certainly the attitude of shy modesty and tenderness with which the figure is represented, as she kneels defenseless and trembling yet secure in her unassailable faith, might seem to indicate this.

The gentle emotion emanating from this work makes one almost overlook its formal qualities: a calm golden light plays over all the simple elements in the picture, painted with rapid, ample brush strokes which recall the great example of El Greco. Yet the loving care with which everything is treated is evident in the soft forms painted in colors limited to a few sober tones. Most striking of all is the masterly diagonal of the composition, repeated and emphasized by the slash of light down the wide stretch of cloth which serves as a link between the little saint and her divine protector, two lonely protagonists in the empty silence of the cell.

140　(L.C.R.)

GERMAN PAINTING
15th-20th Centuries

ALBRECHT DÜRER
Nürnberg 1471—Nürnberg 1528
The Dresden Altarpiece: Madonna and Child
(center panel); *St. Anthony and St. Sebastian*
(side panels, see p. 144)

Tempera on canvas; 46″ x 38″ (center panel);
44⅞″ x 17¾″ (side panels).
Inv. no. 1869

ALBRECHT DÜRER. *The Dresden Altarpiece.*　　　　　　*p. 143–144*

Dürer painted only the central section of this triptych commissioned in 1496 by Frederick the Wise, Elector of Saxony, for the castle chapel at Wittenberg.

The Italianate forms often remarked upon here in reality no more than recall Bramantino or Schiavone. Behind the foreground group, the extensive interior stretching through the open door on the left, showing the workshop with Joseph at work in it, and opening through the window on the right onto a quiet, deserted street at the edge of a town, is almost scrupulously Northern. The jeweled crown itself is Flemish in taste, and the putti which hover around it—more like flying insects than angels—have hard, expressionless faces, similar to the disagreeable face of the sleeping Child, unaware of the watchful, adoring Mother's apprehensions. The dark wall on the left, like a wing in a theatre, and the bright wall opposite, contain—almost constrict—the central group. The illuminated book and small stand, as also the harsh, sculptured folds of cloth and the cushion supporting the Infant are treated three-dimensionally: they are blocks projected in the window embrasure opening onto the outside world, with the sense of distance created by the indoor scene behind, resulting in an immediate dramatic contrast.

Opinion is divided over the side panels (p. 146). Added later, probably in 1503-4, they are thought to be studio works, or at least partially by Cranach, who is known to have worked at the Wittenberg court after 1505. The doubts arise because of a certain hesitancy of execution (pentimenti), and a weakness of composition in the figures, but most of all because of the strange overcrowding of objects and creatures (a real *horror vacui*) in the limited areas in both pictures above and below the figures of the two saints: the angels which literally blot out the sky above, and the still-lifes on the foreground shelves that form extensions of the surface supporting the sleeping Child in the central section. The overall effect of the work indicates a collaboration of assistants, but cannot be identified as the work of any distinctive artist. The relation between the two side panels is altogether too unsure. Unconventional as they are, however—although Dürer could never be said to have been tied to set formulas!—they provide a perfectly adequate complement to this youthful work. Outside the dividing walls which frame the central group in the middle panel, in a small world beyond time and space, a wise man in a cloak and a naked young man turn devoutly toward the Mother watching with painful anxiety over her Child. Four profoundly human figures, a few humble objects, a simple room, and the flight of joyless little angels are already presentiments of the tragic sacrifice. (L.C.R.)

ALBRECHT DÜRER. *Portrait of a Young Man.*　　　　　　*p. 145*

The sitter of this forceful portrait has been traditionally identified as the painter Bernaert van Orley, whom Dürer would have met and sketched during his trip to Flanders in 1521. Cetainly painted after that date, the portrait belongs to his group of non-fullface portraits, and reflects the integration of his recently acquired experience with that of the past, especially his contact with Renaissance Humanism during his early visits to Italy (his return to the Germanic idiom and spiky graphic style of his youth having ended around 1520). The deep artistic culture of the great German master, and his meditations on history and philosophy come out with marvelous immediacy in this portrait, which is both peculiarly alive and expressive, and at the same time conveys "ideal" ethical and spiritual values.

His deliberate imitation of the great Flemish portraitists of around 1520-25 has

ALBRECHT DÜRER
Nürnberg 1471—Nürnberg 1528
Portrait of a Young Man
Oil on panel; 17⅞" x 12⅖".
Signed with monogram at top center.
Inv. no. 1871

even led some critics to question whether it was actually Dürer who painted this portrait. Indeed, comparison with an apparently somewhat similar portrait—the same soft hat, the cape with fur collar, the short, fair hair, the small folds on the white shirt—in the *Portrait of an Unknown Man* in the Prado, which bears the date 1524, confirms the substantial diversity of inspiration: but not, in our opinion, a different hand. In contrast to the imperious, wrathful authority and conscious, stubborn strength of the sitter in the Madrid portrait, the one in Dresden conveys a strength just as intense, yet spiritual, calm, abstracted, almost sorrowful—the unforgettable blue-green eyes afire with some noble, distant, probably unattainable dream. (L.C.R.)

LUCAS CRANACH THE ELDER
Kronach 1472—Weimar 1553
Duke Henry the Pious (1514)
Oil on panel, transferred to canvas; 72½" x 32½".
Inv. no. 1906 G

LUCAS CRANACH THE ELDER
Kronach 1472—Weimar 1553
Duchess Catherine of Mecklenburg
Oil on panel, transferred to canvas; 72½" x 32½".
Inscribed lower left with winged serpent, the monogram L C, and the date 1514. Pendant to the preceding picture.
Inv. 1906 H

LUCAS CRANACH THE ELDER. *Duke Henry the Pious.*

Every aspect of the figure of the young duke—one of Martin Luther's early sympathizers—is painted with a wealth of ornamental detail. Every shape and pattern of the clothing—from the wreath of pinks on his head to the tassels below the knees—becomes a sort of abstract decoration in a style more often associated with coats of arms and heraldic symbols. Bounded by the firm parallel edges of the picture, great swirling folds of cloth billow out and mass together in a series of beautiful shapes. These shapes define the outline of the Duke's slim body, enveloping him as if in a shining golden cuirass and giving him the appearance of some huge, fully armored insect. The whole manner of the painting gives the impression that it is not so much an attempt at "truthful" portrayal as a deliberately abstract exercise in decoration, so that all the actual ornamental elements like the chain necklace, the tinkling gold orbs around the elbows and the crescent-shaped metal plaques on the upper legs merge into the swirling intricacy of the whole design. Even the precious gold hilt of the duke's dagger and the greyhound at his side become part of the great pattern, only incidentally retaining a semblance of descriptive, episodic significance, adding a touch of realistic detail to the composition.

In spite of the triangular pyramid formed in the upper segment of the broad shoulders of the duke, the whole balance of the picture is precarious, caught in an instant of suspended animation.

Another portrait of the Duke, showing him older and bearded (1537), was destroyed in the bombing of the Dresden gallery during the Second World War. (L.C.R.)

LUCAS CRANACH THE ELDER. *Duchess Catherine of Mecklenburg.*

This portrait of the Duchess, standing still and composed—like a fluted column—with her robes hanging heavily about her, contrasts strangely with the fanciful image of her husband. Her pose is traditional, as is her sumptuous dress, perfect in the elaborate cut and studied design of the rich brocade, and the rigorous symmetry of the ornaments and jewelry in a series of heraldic symbols. There is only one formal similarity between this portrait and that of her husband—in this exquisite pair of early works by the artist—the slanting cascade of plumes framing the cold, astute face of Catherine corresponding to the flowered headgear worn by the Duke.

146 (L.C.R.)

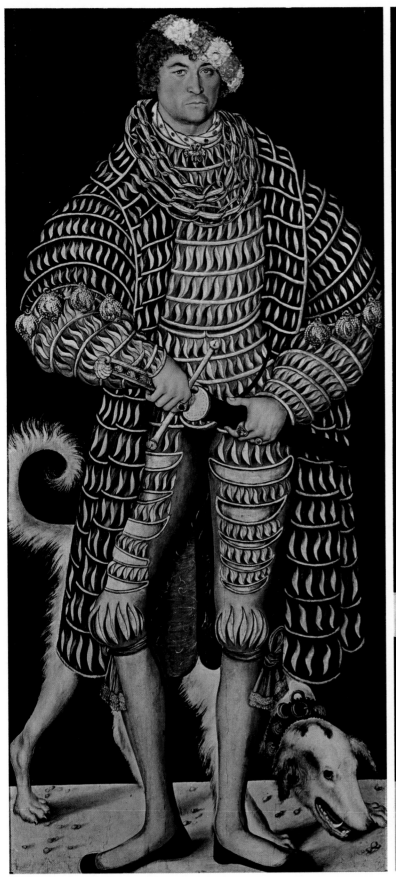

LUCAS CRANACH THE ELDER
Kronach 1472—Weimar 1553
Martyrdom of St. Catherine, center panel of an
altarpiece
Oil on panel; 49⅝" x 54¼".
Signed and dated below, center: L C 1506
Inv. 1906

LUCAS CRANACH THE ELDER. *Martyrdom of St. Catherine.*

This painting, the center panel of an altarpiece, is dated 1506. The side panels are traditional in composition, showing a series of saints, yet clearly having an explicitly ornamental function as indicated by their rich clothes and elaborate hair styles, the figures standing out like columns against the wide sweep of hills and valleys in the background.

By contrast the central panel is far from a typical representation, comprising a mass of figures, elements of landscape and natural detail, all pressing around the still, calm figure of the saint. She kneels, beautiful, elegant and unperturbed, amidst the riotous but carefully balanced throng pushing forward towards the great wheel. The elegant, foppish figure of the executioner and all the bystanders in the group behind him are bathed in bright light from the clear sky on the left of the picture; but over the group on the right hang dark threatening clouds torn apart by a breaking storm of hail and lightning. Yet this does not disturb the colorful pattern formed by the elegant clothes, and the mutilated heads, and the great wheel itself which, though a dreadful instrument of torture, seems an oddly homely and simple object. (L.C.R.)

HANS HOLBEIN THE YOUNGER. *Thomas Godsalve and his Son John.* p. 150

As inscribed in the top left-hand corner, painted in 1528 during a first, short trip to England, this picture shows the notary Thomas Godsalve of Norwich, aged 47, signing his name on a sheet of paper on the table which serves both as the base of the composition, and as a support for the figures of Thomas, flanked a little behind by his son John. Holbein painted another portrait of John some ten years later, with his wife Elisabeth Widmerpole (Philadelphia, and the Reinhardt Collection in Winterthur), after he in turn had come to work at the English court.

In this early double portrait the two figures, so similar and yet so surprisingly different, are aligned in an identical diagonal, both looking the same way, but, as has been pointed out, with an air of detachment and concentration combined that

HANS HOLBEIN THE YOUNGER
Augsburg 1497—London 1543
Thomas Godsalve and his Son John (1528)
Oil on panel; 13¼" x 14⅛".
Dated above left: "Anno. Dni M.D.XXVIII"
Inv. no. 1889

HANS HOLBEIN THE YOUNGER
Augsburg 1497—London 1543
Charles de Solier, Sieur de Morette (1534–35)
Oil on panel; 36⅜" x 29¾".
Inv. no. 1890

recalls the poses and expressions of donors in church altarpieces. The proximity of the two faces—so different yet so closely related—is deliberate. As often, in future years too, Holbein uses the device not so much to portray character, as to convey, through the sense of repeated rhythms, and the identical points of convergence of the two triangles thus formed—as well as through the iconographical contrast between the two faces—a strong pulse of movement latent in the tight-knit composition. (L.C.R.)

HANS HOLBEIN THE YOUNGER. *Charles de Solier, Sieur de Morette.*
Variously attributed in the past (at one time even to Leonardo!), this portrait has only recently, thanks to a medal mold by Christopher Weiditz, been recognized as a Holbein, and identified as such: it is the French ambassador to England between April 1534 and July 1535. The work can thus be dated definitively from that period—Wenceslaus Hollar's 1647 engraving with the inscription "*Mr. Morette ex collectione Arundeliana*" confirms this.

The powerful figure, drawn as a solid polygonal, multi-faceted block, which sets the pattern for the various later, famous three-quarter length portraits of Henry 151

VIII, conveys commanding strength. Everything helps to bring this out and emphasizes it: the background of dark, vibrant, gleaming velvet; the hard, perfectly symmetrical face; the direct look; the magnificent yet at the same time sober clothes. The effect rests on the precise balance of triangles (cap, chain, puffs of light silk, mustache, arched eyebrows, nose) against the two basic squares, the torso and, more importantly, the face—which forms the focal point of the picture, not only because of the subdued light that seems to flow from it, but because of the strength in it, which brings it vividly to life.

The skillfully managed color contrasts are highly effective. In the predominance of dark colors—matte oil-green and deep, almost black chestnut-brown—the light in the square face appears in marked relief, and the white triangles of silk, the odd flashes of shining gold, animate the whole like a kind of subdued, expressive commentary.

As figure-painting the picture is a supreme work of concentrated vitality, transcending in its remarkable form of stylization, which for sheer virtuosity surpasses its Italian models.

The Gallery's Cabinet of Drawings possesses an important study of the ambassador's head. (L.C.R.)

ANTON RAPHAEL MENGS
Aussig, Bohemia 1728—Rome 1779
Self-Portrait with Red Cloak (1744)
Pastel on paper; 21¾" x 16¼".
Inv. no. 1167

ANTON RAPHAEL MENGS. *Self-Portrait with Red Cloak.*
In 1744, at the age of eighteen, Mengs painted two different self-portraits—the *Self-Portrait with Blue Cloak*, destroyed in the Second World War, and this one—both in pastels, both of head and shoulders only, and showing clearly the influence of similar portraits produced by the famous Rosalba Carriera. Both went into the Dresden Gallery, which possesses a considerable number of his works.

Already conscious of his own importance, Mengs (who later came to be considered by his contemporaries as the finest painter in Europe) conveys a slightly "larger-than-life" image of himself, at once nobly reflective and romantically suggestive. The pose is one he often used in his youth—torso turned to the left, making a solid base for the head, which looks squarely forward, the handsome face framed by soft, wavy hair. If the lost *Self-Portrait* explicitly recalled Raphael, with the cloak hanging over the shoulders in semi-circular folds, this one too (of which there is a second-rate copy in Weimar) reveals traces of the great Italian tradition—especially that of Rome—from which Mengs tried to learn how to achieve his ultimate goal: Beauty. And though not yet formulated theoretically, we already see here his conviction that beauty could be achieved by combining everything in one picture, Raphael's draughtsmanship, Correggio's grace, and Titian's color. (L.C.R.)

JOSEPH HEINTZ THE ELDER. *The Rape of Proserpina.*   *pp. 154–155*
The composition of this crowded mythological scene has been most carefully worked out in two concentric arcs, one above the other. In the upper arc the figures are caught up in a flurry of swirling movement, whereas in the lower arc the exquisitely painted figures are arranged harmoniously—in two separate groups—reflecting the work of the sixteenth-century Venetian painters, and also that of Correggio, which Heintz, a painter at the court of Prague, had studied.

A glimpse of a peaceful landscape is visible in the luminous distance, in the center of the canvas between the foreground where the young nymphs are gathered and the dark threatening mass which hangs like a pall above them, from which Pluto's chariot bursts out in a vortex of horses, bodies and flying drapery. (L.C.R.)

Pp. 154–155
JOSEPH HEINTZ THE ELDER
Basel 1564—Prague 1609
The Rape of Proserpina
Oil on copper; 24¾" x 37".
Inv. no. 1971

CASPAR DAVID FRIEDRICH. *Cross on Mountain Top.*
This painting, also known as *The Altar of Tetschen,* and commissioned for a private chapel, attracted a great deal of attention and varied comment when it was first exhibited in the winter of 1808. Preparatory studies preceded it by quite a few years, leading up to a possibly lost sepia drawing of 1807 which served as a model. The gothicizing frame, designed by Friedrich himself and carved by Karl Gottlob Kühn, contains symbolic motives that fit in to the mood of the altarpiece. The subject—a crucifix at the top of a rocky mountain—became one of the artist's often repeated themes. His romantic vision, steeped in mysticism and seeking to create an image of the infinite, the sublime, the unknown, is realized here for the first time in stylistic terms he was never to abandon. Besides the obvious reference to Calvary, Friedrich's central idea incorporated in this canvas with its tapering forms rising toward a stormy sky is the human condition, the loneliness and frailty of man in the face of the vast and eternal universe. (P.C.S.)

WILHELM LEIBL. *Portrait of a Young Woman.*
Wilhelm Leibl was perhaps the most important artist working in Germany at the   157

EMIL NOLDE (EMIL HANSEN)
Nolde, Schleswig, 1867—Seebüll 1956
Sail Boats on the Yellow Sea (1914)
Oil on canvas; 28¾" x 34½".
Signed at bottom right: Emil Nolde
Inv. no. 2818

end of the nineteenth century, even if his realism, derived from Menzel, appears at times to limit him. This small canvas, which precedes by three years the famous *Three Women in Church* in the Hamburg Kunsthalle—to which it is stylistically related—is free from any concession to naturalism. It grows out of the artist's close study of fifteenth-century art, and he came to be known as the "modern Holbein." Here, as throughout his work, he illustrates qualities of discipline and control which are reflected perhaps more effectively in his drawings; these form a large corpus of remarkable consistency which expresses his belief that "to draw everything is good; to have everything drawn is better." The light tones of the girl's dress and the warm, rosy glow of her cheeks stand out against the dark background. Her pensive, brooding head is very close to that of the youngest of the *Three Women,* and like that one its features are incisively drawn. Notable is the clarity with which the eyes, lips and the folds of the blouse have been recorded. Stripped of superfluous accessories, the portrait is devoid of the redundant details which clutter up and deaden Leibl's more anecdotal or narrative works. (P.C.S.)

EMIL NOLDE. *Sail Boats on the Yellow Sea.*

Throughout his long life—he died in 1956, nearly ninety years old—Nolde remained faithful to the style he first developed, even in his late years when he muted his earlier, all embracing violence of vision, depicting calm seas beneath the tranquil dome of the sky, lightly tracing the outlines of objects in a refined, decorative style reminiscent of Oriental art. This painting, which dates from his most important period of activity, clearly manifests the gestural and chromatic tension of his works, which have a primitive, almost savage impetuosity. Ensor's example, as well as the influence of the artistic innovations of van Gogh, Munch and the Fauvists, all played an important role. Yet Nolde was able to create an exciting, individual style which goes far beyond the experiments of his Expressionist friends. Avoiding any accepted norms, intolerant of discipline, he leaves the space of the composition undefined and unorganized, freely mixing the bright oranges and reds with darker, heavier colors and pale pastel tones. The boats, seen from above as splashes of reflected light and color, move on the small waves, leaving no horizontals but only various diagonals whose sharp angles stress the primitive strength which underlies the whole. (P.C.S.)

LYONEL FEININGER
New York 1871—New York 1956
A Street at Night (1929)
Oil on canvas; 14½″ x 22″.
Signed at bottom left. Feininger
Inv. no. 2736

LYONEL FEININGER. *A Street at Night.*

"All true art is based on or abstracted from a simple imitation of our great master—nature." With this saying, which echoes Goethe's ideas, Feininger defined what was perhaps his deepest conviction on the subject of artistic expression, reflected in this *Street at Night*, on a theme repeated three years later in a version now in the Basle Kunstmuseum. During this period he was working at the Bauhaus in Dessau, in close relationship with Klee, Kandinsky and Jawlensky, who with him formed the "Blue Four" group. His style, after a certain kinship with Futurism and Cubism, became purer and more refined through his contact with the Bauhaus and Walter Gropius, even though, unlike the latter, he never felt the purely architectonic value of forms. While his style may contain geometric undertones his finished compositions could never be reduced to rigidly measured, symmetrical schemes. For instance in this painting of houses at night a soft, glowing light dissolves the various solid planes by manipulating reflections, juxtapositions and sequences of light and shade. Hentzen noted this as a "transparent city," which can therefore be defined as unreal, rigorous and yet at the same time sensitive, with suggestions of romantic leanings. The interpenetration of the incisive shapes across the canvas, as well as their schematic simplification, are close to Cubist conventions, though the way in which they have been adapted and developed is completely personal. Notable also is the fineness and delicacy of color with which this silent, mysterious view has been expressed. (P.C.S.)

160

HISTORY OF THE MUSEUM
AND ITS BUILDING

As its well established reputation suggests, the "*Alte Meister*," or collection of Old Master paintings, is considered the most important part of Dresden's national art collections, known as "*Verband der Staatlichen Kunstsammlungen Dresden.*" This assemblage of art treasures comprises no less than nine collections, originally deriving from the *Kunstkammer* which the Elector Augustus I (1526-1586) founded in his castle in 1560. The *Kunst-* or *Wunderkammern*—galleries of paintings and objects of *vertu*, which usually included bizarre curiosities ranging from stuffed birds or fossils to expensive scientific instruments or rare books and maps—became very popular and widespread during this period, and are characteristic of those formed by the various German princes, such as those of the Elector of Saxony.

However, the Dresden Kunstkammer contained important works of art even during its early years before the seventeenth century—for instance examples by Lucas Cranach and Hans Krell, both of whom worked for the Saxon court, as well as three by Jacopo de'Barbari. In 1687 these masterpieces were joined by Dürer's famous *Adoration*, the *Dresden Altarpiece*, which had been acquired from the Schlosskirche in Wittenberg. The 1658 inventory shows that the Kunstkammer at that time contained a collection of a hundred and eighteen paintings, whose character as a whole is so varied and contradictory as to suggest that they were not bought with any well considered criteria in mind.

It was in the eighteenth century that a greater and more systematically rationalized urge to collect came to be felt in Dresden as in the rest of Europe. It was in fact during the middle of the century, characterized as it was by the refined sophistication of the Dresden court, that the collection attained a prestige and fame which placed it quite securely among those of the richest and most aristocratic courts in Europe.

The credit for acquiring the masterpieces of which Dresden is justifiably proud belongs above all to *cognoscenti* who were also very skilled dealers; also there was a wealth of experience of the political ins and outs of acquiring or exchanging works and the sales between dealers in the most important European cities, particularly in the north; and added to this there were even gifts from artists, their generosity, or common sense, inspired by the enlightened patronage of the Saxon court.

At the end of the seventeenth century eleven very important paintings, including a Rubens, were bought in Venice; thirty years before eighteen Cranachs had been acquired, joining a collection which could already boast of many major artists, among whom there were Dürer, Bronzino and Jacopo de'Barbari. In 1699 Augustus II acquired Giorgione's famous *Venus*, finished by Titian, through the antiquary Le Roy, from whom he also bought some paintings by Jacopo Bassano, Guido Reni, Claude Lorrain and four by Philips Wouwerman. The first important acquisition of the early eighteenth century consisted of a staggering three hundred and forty-two paintings, which included, amongst various minor artists, painters of the first rank—Rembrandt, Breughel, Gabriel Metsu, Adam Elsheimer, Ruisdael, Gerard Dou and David Teniers.

In 1722 Augustus the Strong had an inventory made of all the paintings which were at that time divided between various castles, churches and the Wunderkammer, and had the second floor of the Judenhof stables reconstructed for use as an art gallery. Thus was born the first real *Gemäldegalerie*, which though separated from 4,700 objects of lesser importance, still contained 1,938 paintings, among which there were some rare masterpieces.

The first keeper and director was Raymond Le Plat, at that time also Architect to the court. He deserves the credit for the acquisition of various paintings of high quality by famous artists—for instance Rubens' copy of Michelangelo's *Leda*, and paintings by artists like Guido Reni, Simon Vouet and others. These years also mark the acquisition of numerous works which, although not by famous artists and far from being masterpieces, are nevertheless important in that they give a complete picture of the age and the schools of painters working at the time. Thus over sixty fifteenth-century Italian paintings were acquired, and about sixty by Dutch masters; a few years later another fifty Italian works were added, as well as some paintings of the French school. In this way the gallery acquired a character which was to have a decisive influence on all its future development. As a whole Dresden does not give one a systematic, all embracing view of the development of different schools, being more the result of the personal taste and choice of the Electors rather than any rational, critical system designed to provide some encyclopedic account of European painting. This character is particularly evident in the way, side-by-side with Flemish and Dutch masterpieces of the seventeenth century, are hung works by minor painters of the same school, artists whose works are represented in hardly any other museums; and yet at the same time one notes the near absence of any English artists and a minimal number of works from before the Renaissance, although at the end of the nineteenth century efforts were made to fill these gaps.

Besides the masterpieces of Northern artists the presence of paintings from the Italian schools is notable. From the fifteenth to the eighteenth centuries all the various schools are represented by works by their most prominent artists—the Florentine by Fra Angelico, Botticelli, Lorenzo di Credi, and Andrea del Sarto; the Bolognese by the Carracci, Guido Reni, Domenichino, Guercino and Crespi; Umbria by Pinturicchio; Ferrara and Parma by Cosimo Tura, Correggio, Francesco del Cossa, Ercole de'Roberti and Parmigianino; the Neapolitan school by Salvator Rosa, Luca Giordano and Francesco Solimena; not to mention Mantegna or Raphael or the Venetian school with some of the best works by Titian, Tintoretto, Giorgione, Lorenzo Lotto, Bellini, Tiepolo and the *vedutisti* Canaletto and Bellotto.

The Dresden Gallery was, however, to reach the height of its artistic splendor during the reign of King Frederick Augustus III, who came to the throne in 1733 and under whom the Prime Minister, Count Brühl, was given charge of the collection and the job of collecting new works, a commission which he personally fulfilled with great success. His agents and dealers were sent to all the major capitals of Europe, particularly to the centers of the art market in Germany, Holland and Paris; meanwhile Luigi Crespi worked for him in Bologna and A. M. Zanetti in Venice, while Count Francesco Algarotti, art theorist and historian, collected paintings for him all over Italy.

The new king, a man of great refinement, had a particular preference for Italian art. Between 1738 and 1743 over one hundred and seventy canvases by Italian masters were added to the collection. While these were obviously not all masterpieces, they did contain among their number works by such masters as Veronese, Bassano, and Guercino; and in addition to these, two by Ribera, and an early El Greco. However, the most sensational acquisition came after long and delicate negotiations towards the end of 1746, when one hundred of the best paintings from the collection of Francesco III d'Este, Duke of Modena were bought. Among this number there are such famous paintings as Veronese's *The Cuccina Family*, four Correggio altarpieces, Titian's *Tribute Money*, Holbein's *Charles de Solier, Sieur de Morette* (once attributed to Leonardo), and Rubens' *St. Jerome*. Apart from these there are three paintings by Velazquez, and others by Andrea del Sarto, the Carracci, Guido Reni, Tintoretto, Parmigianino and several more of Titian's work, as well as a very valuable collection of works by minor artists of the Emilian and Tuscan schools.

In 1754, less than ten years later, came the Gallery's best known single acquisition, Raphael's *Sistine Madonna*, which was sold for twenty thousand ducats by the monks of the monastery of San Sisto in Piacenza directly to Augustus III, and replaced in its original setting with a copy by Nogari.

A few years previously other works of great value had joined the Dresden Gallery, which by 1754 contained one thousand four hundred and forty-six paintings. Among these there were two predella panels by Ercole de'Roberti, acquired in Italy by P. Guarienti; the *Annunciation* by Francesco del Cossa, a gift from Luigi Crespi; and the *Madonna of the Rose* by Parmigianino. Most important was the complete Wallenstein collection from Leipzig, which contained among others Jan Vermeer's famous canvas *Dalla Mezzana* (*The Procuress*), as well as some by Hals and a van Dyck. From the Bohemian Imperial Galleries came Rubens' *Boar Hunt* and Tintoretto's *The Liberation of Arsinoë*, Bartolomeo Veneto's *Salome*, a genre scene by Valentin de Boullogne, van Dyck's *Henrietta of France*, Metsy's *The Money Lenders* and a *Crucifixion* by Guido Reni.

Works by Domenico Feti came from Prague; from the Carignan estate in Paris came two Rembrandts—*Saskia Holding a Red Carnation* and the *Self-Portrait with Saskia*. Also from the same source came some Poussins and a Murillo. Other important acquisitions were made in Holland and Flanders.

Overriding financial problems and the outbreak of the Seven Years War a short while after in 1756 stopped the heavy flow of works into the collection; in 1759, except for a few rare examples, this was moved into the castle of Königstein where it remained until the end of the war. Two years later, first in French and a few years after in German, the first catalogue of the collection, drawn up by J. A. Riedel, came out, listing all the surviving works, many of which had suffered near irreparable damage. In fact, it was at this stage that the process of restoration which was to last throughout the rest of the eighteenth and the nineteenth centuries began, a process which did not necessarily restore the damaged works to their original beauty and perfection of color, leaving instead traces of clumsy retouching which are unfortunately very obvious today.

The job of supervising and coordinating the delicate operation of conservation and restoration fell to an Italian from Rome, Pietro Palmaroli, who was called to Dresden in 1826. He above all deserves the credit for the restoration and conservation of Raphael's *Sistine Madonna*.

It was only towards the end of the nineteenth century that any consistent attempt at collecting was resumed. The Spanish school is represented by some beautiful works, among which there are the paintings by Murillo and Zurbaran which were bought in London from the collection of Louis-Philippe of France in 1854; and a few years later came a Lorenzi di Credi. But, most importantly, there were the four predella panels by Botticelli illustrating the life of St. Zenobius, bought in 1868; Antonello da Messina's famous *St. Sebastian* bought in 1873, and, three years later, Mantegna's *Holy Family*.

In the second half of the century, after the bourgeois revolution of 1848–9, the idea of creating a new and different part of the gallery devoted to contemporary art picked up more and more support. This was originally housed in the same buildings as the "*Alte Meister*" collections; however the lack of space, a problem made more acute by this new collection, soon reached the point of requiring an immediate and effective solution. So in 1847, under the direction of the architect Gottfried Semper, work began on the construction of a new building for the collection at the Zwinger. This new building—finished eight years later in 1855—was still not big enough to house the complete collection, gathered as it had been for nearly three centuries by the Electors of Saxony. At the opening two thousand two hundred works were exhibited, while a good seven hundred were kept in reserve, many of which were later unfortunately auctioned. It was only in 1931 that the "Neue Meister," containing works by modern artists which are now exhibited in the Albertinum, became an independent entity separate from the "Alte Meister."

Another date of fundamental importance in the history of the museum is 1882, when the erudite art historian Karl Woermann became its director. With him in particular lies the credit for the new catalogue, based on new principles and drawn up along revolutionary lines and reattributing many works to different artists. He was also responsible for the adoption, from these years onwards, of a more diversified approach to collecting, preferring to buy works in order to complete existing examples of a particular school or period rather than for their independent merit or some personal preference.

Between the last years of the nineteenth century and the first years of the twentieth, some important acquisitions were made, despite financial difficulties: Cosimo Tura's *St. Sebastian*; *The Pietà* by the Master of the Housebook; two canvases by Cranach of *Duke Henry the Good* and *The Duchess Caterina von Mecklenburg*; a Reynolds and a Murillo. And throughout this time the need to add to and develop the section devoted to modern art deprived the Old Masters of much of the attention they would have otherwise received. In any case after the First World War the Gallery was continuously adding new works to itself—two beautiful paintings by Tiepolo, paintings by Lorenzo Costa (*The Madonna Reading*), Francia, Hans Baldung (*Mucius Scaevola*), five by Cranach including his *Earthly Paradise*, and others by less important artists.

The Second World War had the effect of dividing up Dresden's artistic treasures, some of which went, for reasons of security, to castles scattered all over the country; in the period after the war many of these masterpieces disappeared without trace. The works remaining in the Gallery of the Zwinger were destroyed, together with the museum, in the Allied bombing raid on the 13th of February 1945; in all about two hundred works were lost, including those which had been collected together in a convoy in a last, desperate attempt to take them to the Terrassenufer.

However, in 1945 one thousand two hundred and forty works from the collection were still in existence, some temporarily stored in Moscow (seven hundred and seventy-two), some in Kiev and the rest in Leningrad. Here they were successfully restored, and returned in 1955 to Dresden where in the meanwhile work had begun on the rebuilding of Semper's museum, keeping close to the original designs, while at the same time modifying the interior layout, in particular of the rooms and the windows, which were enlarged to allow in extra light. On the 3rd of June 1956 the Gallery was partly re-opened to the public, and by the 31st of October 1960 the reconstruction of the museum as a whole was complete.

GROUND FLOOR

1. Tapestry room
2, 3. 16th-century Italian Art

I Entrance

IV Information office

II/XI General services

FIRST FLOOR

4. Document room (history of the
   museum)
5, 6, 7, 8, 9, 10, 11. 17th-Century
Flemish and Dutch Art
12. German, Flemish, and Dutch
   Primitives
13. 17th-century French Art
14, 15, 16, 17. 17th-century Italian Art
18, 19, 20. 15th- and 16th-century Italian
   Art and documentation of restoration
   work

XII Bar

XIII Bookstore

SECOND FLOOR

22. Pastels
23. 18th-century French Art
24, 25, 26, 27, 28. 18th-century Italian
   Art
29, 30, 31, 17th-century Spanish Art
32, 33, 34, 35, 36, 37. 17th- and 18th-
   century German Art

PLAN OF THE BUILDING

Alte Meister Galleries

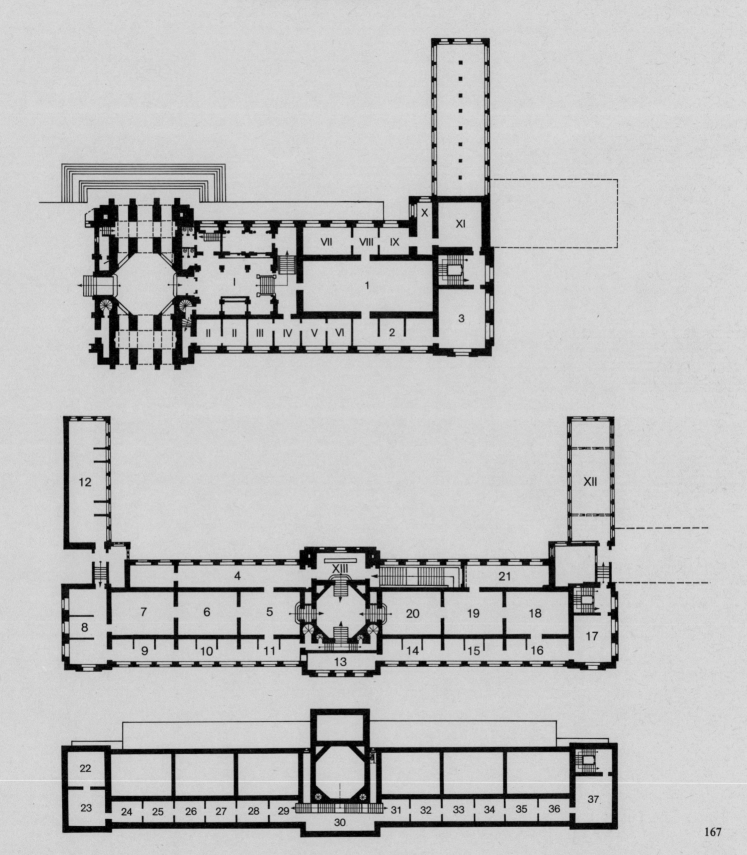

SCHÄFER, WILHELM
Historisch-kritischer Catalog der Königlichen Gemälde-Galerie zu Dresden Dresden, 1876.

WOERMANN, KARL
Katalog der Königlichen Gemäldegalerie zu Dresden, Dresden, 1887.

SINGER, HANS WOLFGANG
Dresden. 1. Die Kgl. Gemälde-Galerie (Preface by Karl Woermann), Berlin, Leipzig, 1906.

POSSE, HANS
Die Gemäldegalerie zu Dresden, Berlin, Dresden; 1 part: *Alte Meister*, 1920; 2 part: *Neuere Meister*, 1921.

POSSE, HANS
Die Staatliche Gemäldegalerie zu Dresden. Vollständiges beschreibendes Verzeichnis der älteren Gemälde. Erste Abteilung: Die romanischen Länder. Italien, Spanien, Frankreich und Russland. Dresden, Berlin 1930.

BACHMANN, MANFRED; MENZ, HENNER
Galeria de pintura de Dresde. Alte Meister, Madrid, 1969.
Die Staatliche Gemäldegalerie zu Dresden. Katalog der modernen Galerie (Introduction by Hans Posse), Dresden-Berlin, 1930.

SEYDEWITZ, RUTH UND MAX
Das Dresdener Galeriebuch, 400 Jahre Dresdener Gemäldegalerie, 1 edition: Dresden, 1957.

RUDLOFF-HILLE, GERTRUD
Gemäldegalerie Dresda, Novara, 1960.

MENZ, HENNER
Die Dresdener Gemäldegalerie, Leipzig, 1º vol.: *Italienische, spanische und französische Meister*, 1961; 2º vol.: *Niederländische, deutsche und englische Meister*, 1962.

MENZ, HENNER
The Dresden Gallery, New York, 1962.

EBERT, HANS
Kriegsverluste der Dresdener Gemäldegalerie. Vernichtete und vermisste Werke, Dresden, 1963.
Gemäldegalerie Neue Meister (Catalog), 4ª edizione: Dresden, 1975.
Gemäldegalerie Dresden. Alte Meister (Catalog), 16ª edizione: Dresden, 1974.

ZIMMERMANN, HORST
Dresdner Galerie Neue Meister, Leipzig, 1964.

ALPATOW, MICHAEL W.
Die Dresdener Galerie. Alte Meister (with the collaboration of Katharina Scheinfu and Irina Danilowa), Dresden, 1966.

SEYDEWITZ, MAX
Die Dresdener Gemäldegalerie. Alte und Neue Meister, Leipzig, 1967.

BACHMANN, MANFRED; MENZ, HENNER
Pinacoteca di Dresda, Milan, 1970

INDEX OF ILLUSTRATIONS

INDEX OF NAMES

The numbers in italics refer to names cited in the captions.